A SHORT TREATISE

ON

HINDU LAW

Owing to the antiquity and rarity of this book, certain pages are regrettably absent, and readability is compromised due to the blurring of the original text. If you possess any insights regarding the availability of these missing sections, kindly inform us. Your assistance is crucial in ensuring the completion of this significant work for the benefit of future generations.

A SHORT TREATISE

ON

HINDU LAW:

AS ADMINISTERED

IN THE COURTS OF BRITISH INDIA

HERBERT COWELL

GYAN

Published by

Gyan Publishing House
5, Ansari Road
Daryaganj, New Delhi-110002
Phone: 011-47034999, 9811692060
E-mail: books@gyanbooks.com

Distribution Network
gyanbooks.com
India, USA, Canada, UK, Australia

ISBN: 978-93-7169-465-0 (PB)

First Published, 1895

2nd Impression 2025

Printed at: Gyan Press, Delhi.

**A SHORT TREATISE ON HINDU LAW:
AS ADMINISTERED IN THE COURTS OF BRITISH INDIA**

Author: HERBERT COWELL

A SHORT TREATISE

ON

HINDU LAW.

A SHORT TREATISE

ON

HINDU LAW

AS ADMINISTERED

IN THE COURTS OF BRITISH INDIA.

BY

HERBERT COWELL,

MIDDLE TEMPLE, BARRISTER-AT-LAW,

AUTHOR OF "THE HISTORY AND CONSTITUTION OF THE COURTS AND LEGISLATIVE AUTHORITIES IN INDIA."

1895.

PREFACE.

THESE outlines of Hindu Law are published to supply the recognised need of a text book for students which shall comprise within reasonable limits a view of the whole subject. The book is founded partly on my Tagore Law Lectures of 1870 and 1871, partly on lectures addressed by me to the students of the Inns of Court about two years ago. I have thought it desirable to treat the very special subjects of adoption and succession in strict relation to the ancient authorities, as well as to decided cases; but have stated the law as to the existence and exercise of proprietary rights at the present day from the actual decisions on those subjects. The subject is too complicated to be compressed within the ordinary limits of a student's manual, and it is hoped that in the following pages clearness has not been sacrificed to brevity.

H. C.

5, CROWN OFFICE ROW, TEMPLE,
16*th September*, 1895.

TABLE OF CASES.

TABLE OF CONTENTS.

CHAPTER IV.

PAGE

THE JOINT ESTATE.—POWER OF ALIENATION.—THE MANAGER.

CHAPTER V.

THE JOINT ESTATE.—POWER OF ALIENATION.—THE COPARCENER.

CHAPTER VI.

THE JOINT ESTATE.—PARTITION.

CHAPTER VII.

THE JOINT ESTATE.—PARTITION.

CHAPTER VIII.

THE WIDOW'S ESTATE.

CHAPTER IX.

PAGE

THE LAW OF ALIENATION.—GIFTS.

CHAPTER X.

THE MEMBERS OF THE JOINT FAMILY—THEIR CIVIL STATUS.

CHAPTER XI.

THE LAW OF WILLS.

CHAPTER XII.

RELIGIOUS ENDOWNMENTS.

CHAPTER XIII.

THE RITE AND CONTRACT OF ADOPTION.

PAGE

CHAPTER XIV.

ADOPTION.—WHO MAY ADOPT.

CHAPTER XV.

ADOPTION.—WHO MAY BE ADOPTED.

CHAPTER XVI.

THE EFFECT OF ADOPTION.

CHAPTER XVII.

THE LAW OF SUCCESSION.

CHAPTER XVIII.

THE LAW OF INHERITANCE.

CHAPTER XIX.

PAGE

ON LINEAL INHERITANCE.

CHAPTER XX.

ON COLLATERAL INHERITANCE.

CHAPTER XXI.

ON EXCLUSION FROM INHERITANCE.

CHAPTER I.

SOURCES OF HINDU LAW.

Title of Hindus to their own laws—Imperial and local Statutes to that effect—On whom Hindu law obligatory—Effect of conversion—Sources of Hindu law as now administered—Legislation—Case law—Usage—Ancient authorities—Five schools of law—Their special authorities—To whom applicable.

AN Act of Parliament passed in 1781 (21 Geo. III. c. 70, s. 17) provides with regard to Hindus that their inheritance and succession shall be determined by their own laws, and that regard shall be had to their civil and religious usages. Prior to that date the same policy of securing to Hindus their own laws and usages had been followed in the 23rd rule of Warren Hastings's plan for the administration of justice, which was drawn up in 1772. The Act of 1781 only applied to Bengal, but when the Recorders' Courts were established by Parliament in Madras and Bombay in 1797, the same rights were secured to the Hindus in those Presidencies. Local regulations in the three Presidencies (*a*) enacted to the same effect.

All Hindus within the British Empire are entitled to have their own laws and usages administered to them to the extent prescribed by the foregoing legislation. Those laws can only be altered by special legislation intended to be applicable to Hindus—*e.g.*, the Hindu Wills Act, the contract code, the provisions relating to the age of majority, remarriage of widows, and the like. Further, those laws are obligatory only on those

(*a*) Bengal Regulation IV. of 1793, s. 15.
Madras Regulation III. of 1802.
Bombay Regulation IV. of 1799.

who are Hindus both by birth and religion. If a Hindu abjures his own religion and is converted to another, so that he ceases to be Hindu in religion as well as in race, he will be governed by the personal laws and usages of the class with which he has associated himself (*a*). That law as regards inheritance and succession would ordinarily be as laid down in the Indian Succession Act, 1865.

The sources of the laws administered to Hindus by the Courts in British India as those laws have been ascertained during more than a century of administration are as follows:—

First in authority is direct legislation. The local statute law now existing in British India consists firstly of

Bengal regulations from 1793—1834.

Madras regulations from 1802—1834.

Bombay regulations from 1827—1834.

Secondly, there is a body of Acts from 1834 to 1861 passed by the Governor-General in Council for the whole of India established by an Act of Parliament passed in 1833.

Thirdly, there is a further body of Acts passed by the Governor-General in Council under the Indian Councils Act of 1861, which begin in 1862, and are continued to the present date.

Fourthly, there are Acts passed by the local legislative Councils of Bengal, Madras, and Bombay which also begin in 1862; by the Local Council for the North-West Provinces and Oudh which was established in 1886; and there are also local regulations passed by the Governor-General in Council under 33 Vict. c. 3.

The next source of the Hindu law actually administered in British India is to be found in the reports of decided case . Those decisions were from 1793, or perhaps earlier, given by English judges, who were originally mere mouthpieces of the pundits attached to their Courts whom they were bound to

(*a*) See Abraham *v.* Abraham, 1 S. W. R. P.C., 1. Myna Boyee *v.* Ootaram, 8 Moore, I. A., 400.

consult. Later the pundits were made to cite authorities, and submit them for the consideration of the Courts. In Western and Northern India the Courts also obtained evidence as to usage from the heads of castes. By Act XI. of 1864 the pundits were abolished as official referees of the Court, and the Hindu law has since been declared by the Courts on authorities which are now accessible to all. A body of case law, the result of the administration of Hindu law for more than a century, is at the present day the main source, both to student and practitioner, of Hindu law as now applied. The decisions of the Privy Council must be accepted as the final adjudication on all disputed points. Next in authority are the decisions of Full Benches of the various High Courts.

A third source is to be found in immemorial usage. "Clear proof of usage will outweigh the written text of the law" (*a*). It must specially be appealed to in the case of Sikhs, Jats, and Jains (*b*). Amongst those governed by the ordinary Hindu law, the custom which overrides it is either local or family custom. In order to be valid, it must be ancient and invariable, definite and clearly proved (*c*). Family custom cannot arise where the family or estate is modern. If a custom is discontinued, it is at an end, and cannot be revived. It may be different from the law of the surrounding district, but must not be immoral or contrary to public policy.

The last source of Hindu law, which is, however, the original basis on which all decided cases rest, is to be found in the ancient authorities, which must still be consulted upon any point not yet illustrated by judicial decision. These authorities are the *Smritis*—*i.e.*, recollections handed down by the Rishis or sages of antiquity, the Code of Menu, the works of Yajnavalkya, Narada, and others. Practically the commentaries on

(*a*) The Ramnad case, 1 Beng. L. R. P.C., 1, 12.
(*b*) Sheo Singh Rai *v.* Dakho, L. R. 5 I. A., 87, 107.
(*c*) Ramalakshmi *v.* Sivananantha, 12 Beng. L. R. P.C., 396.

these works are the starting point of Hindu law, the chief of which are the Mitakshara, by Vijnanesvara, and the Dayabhaga, by Jimutavahana. The former is the basis of Hindu law in all the schools; it is supreme in the province of Benares and in the South and West of India, and is followed with slight variations in other provinces. In Bombay it is supplemented and modified by the Vyavahara Mayukha. In Mithila, *i.e.*, Tirhoot and North Behar, by the Vivada Chintamoni. In Bengal alone it is controlled, though not totally superseded, by the Dayabhaga, which is there accepted as paramount on all points in which it differs from the Mitakshara. The date of the Mitakshara is the 11th century; of the Dayabhaga some three centuries later. These and other commentaries are to be preferred as authorities to the ancient texts (*a*). Jagannatha's Digest, translated by Mr. Colebrooke, is also a work of high authority on the Dayabhaga system of Hindu law (*b*).

There are five schools of Hindu law: the Bengal, Mithila, Benares, Maharashtra, and Dravida. The last four, however, only differ so far as they modify the Mitakshara, and the variations between them are not radical. For most purposes it may be considered that there are only two schools, those of the Mitakshara and the Dayabhaga, the differences between which are vital, and pervade—(1) the joint family system, (2) the order of succession and inheritance, (3) the practice of adoption.

The special authorities of each school are the Smriti Chandrika, by Devanda Bhatta, in the Dravida school; the Vyavahara Mayukha by Nilakantha and the Viramitrodaya, in the Maharashtra; the Vivada Chintamoni, by Vachespati Misra, in the Mithila. These modify in those schools the Mitakshara, the work of Vijnanesvara, which is the great Benares authority. In Bengal, the Dayabhaga, the work of Jimutavahana, supersedes

(*a*) The Ramnad case, 10 Suth. W. R. P.C., 17.

(*b*) Per Dwarkanath Mitter, J., in Kery Kolitani *v.* Moneeram, 13 Beng. L. R., 50.

the Mitakshara on points where they differ; the Dayatatwa, by Raghunandana, and Daya Krama Sangraha, by Sri Krishna Tarkalanhara, are also leading authorities in the same province.

It must be observed that Hindus can change the school of law by which they will be governed as readily as they can change their religion. The question is in all cases one of intention, as manifested by the character of the purohits, ceremonies, and usages which they or their descendants retain about them (*a*). The presumption is always in favour of a Hindu retaining the shasters of his birth, and his intention to change them must be clearly proved. Hindu law is strictly a personal law, although locality is often a safe test as to the school of personal law which governs a particular case.

(*a*) Rutcheeputty Jha *v.* Rajunda Narain Rae, 2 Moore, I. A., 132. See also Rany Srimutty Dibeah *v.* Rany Koond Luta, 4 Moore, I. A., 292.

CHAPTER II.

CO-OWNERSHIP AND ITS VARIOUS RIGHTS.

Joint family—Caste—Definition of co-ownership under the Mitakshara—Who are co-owners—Origin and completion of coparcener's title—Nature of coparcener's right to a share—Effect of partition on title—Co-ownership under the Dayabhaga—Separate title of each coparcener to his share—Effect of partition—Comparison of Mitakshara, Dayabhaga, and English coparceners—Relative rights of co-owners under the Mitakshara—Management of the joint estate—Rights of the father under the Bengal and Mitakshara schools—Powers of the manager—Right to account against him—Rights of maintenance—(1) Male members of the family; (2) Wife; (3) Widow; (4) Son's wife and widow; (5) Mother and grandmother.

THE Hindu family, joint in food, worship and estate, is the main characteristic of the Hindu community, which remains throughout most of India as it was in the time of Menu, an aggregation of families rather than of individuals. Beyond the family there is the caste system. In some parts of India castes are very numerous. The four historic and well-known divisions are the Brahmana, the Kshatriya, the Vaisya, and the Sudra. The three higher stand in many respects on a common footing, since by a succession of religious ceremonies their members attain regeneration. Sudras are the servants of the other classes. The only regenerating ceremony for a Sudra or for a woman of any caste is that of marriage.

Of the joint family, its commensality need not be referred to, and its joint worship will be treated later on.

Co-ownership by a Hindu family is the basis of Hindu society, and the first subject with which Hindu law deals. The

Mitakshara and Dayabhaga systems differ radically with regard to it. The best definition of Mitakshara co-ownership is that given by Lord Westbury (*a*). "According to the true notion of an undivided family, no individual member of that family whilst it remains undivided can predicate of the joint undivided property that he, that particular member, has a certain definite share. The proceeds of undivided property must be brought according to the theory of an undivided family to the common chest or purse, and then dealt with according to the modes of enjoyment of the members of an undivided family. But when the members of an undivided family agree among themselves with regard to particular property that it shall thenceforth be the subject of ownership in certain definite shares, then the character of undivided property and joint enjoyment is taken away from the subject-matter so agreed to be dealt with; and in the estate each member has thenceforth a definite and certain share which he may claim a right to receive and to enjoy in severalty, although the property itself has not been actually severed and divided."

Co-ownership is not vested in all the members of a joint family. The joint family consists of all the descendants, male and female, of a married pair, say the original sole owner of an ancestral estate and his wife. The coparceners include only the male descendants to the fourth generation, and thus consist of the man himself, his sons, grandsons, and great grandsons. This coparcenary title arises at birth; it is called an inchoate title, for it is not a complete one till partition. It represents a variable interest, being diminished by every successive birth of a male member of the family within three generations from the original owner, and being increased by every successive death of such coparcener. Each parcener has this inchoate and variable title fastened on the whole property so long as it remains joint.

(*a*) Appoovier *v.* Rama Subba Aiyan, 8 Suth. W. R. P.C., 1; s. c. 11 Moore, I. A., 75.

The right of a parcener to a share is contingent upon a partition being made. Not every parcener has a right to partition at any given moment. Those in the same degree, or their representatives, if dead, can compel partition with one another and with their father if he holds separately from his collaterals. On a partition being made the shares are allotted, and then each allottee holds his share separately from those with whom he has partitioned, but joint with his male lineal descendants as far as great grandsons. So long as no partition takes place the co-ownership is vested in all the coparceners, whose numbers, of course, vary with the births and deaths which take place; and there is no such thing until partition as inheritance by any individual coparcener. The law of inheritance only steps in to regulate the amount of the share which will be taken whenever a partition is come to. Brothers will share equally, but if one is dead his representatives, however numerous, will only take jointly between them the share of the deceased, succession being *per stirpes* and not *per capita.*

Co-ownership, as recognised by the Dayabhaga, is entirely different. It is not aggregate, but fractional ownership. The co-owners hold the estate in common, each having a separate title to a share. While the father lives he is absolute owner of the ancestral as well as his self-acquired estate. The sons have no inchoate title therein by birth. Their title accrues at his death. Each takes a separate title to a definite but unascertained portion of the estate. Joint estate, according to the Bengal school, does not mean that each coparcener has a title to the whole. It means that he has title to a definite share, but that the estate is not yet divided, so that the particular portion of property which represents his share is not yet allotted to him. Each coparcener, so soon as his title accrues, holds a separate title. Partition is the division of the estate, not of the title thereto, which was always a divided one. There is no succession by survivorship. The title of each being separate descends by the law of inheritance. Coparceners under the Bengal school resemble tenants in common under English law, except that they derive their title by descent, while English tenants in common do not. Mitakshara coparceners resemble English joint tenants in this, that each has the entirety of interest, and each has a right of survivorship. But the inchoate rights vested in the sons by birth, indefinable as estates in the land, but which include a right to maintenance, in some cases a right to call for partition and a right to defeat alienation made without their consent, are peculiar to the Mitakshara. The right of survivorship, moreover, is modified by representation. On a partition it prevails against a brother's widow but not against a brother's male issue.

Thus the aggregate ownership under the Mitakshara is the special feature of Hindu law. The relative rights during the continuance of the joint estate may be summed up as follows :— (1) all coparceners can claim partition, assuming the ancestors above them are dead ; (2) all have rights to maintenance, and rights of maintenance belong also to members of the joint family who are not coparceners ; (3) coparceners can defeat alienation made without their consent ; (4) some have rights of management. Usually it is the father or other principal member of the family who is entitled to the management. In Bengal he is called the Kurta. Some liability to account is enforced ; (5) all acquisitions of property made by any member of the joint family with the use of the joint funds are joint estate. Under the Dayabhaga system the father can do as he pleases with the whole estate, after his death each coparcener can do as he pleases with his share. Accordingly, rights of management and of maintenance are more restricted under that system. With regard to management, the father under the Mitakshara, though he is not as in Bengal absolute proprietor, has a larger power as manager than is possessed by an elder brother after his death. The father's dealings with the joint property will stand unless they contravene law or morality. The annual shrads, investitures with the sacred thread, the marriage of the minor girls of the family, and other religious ceremonies, are under the supervision of any manager. With regard to his dealings with the joint estate for these purposes, the rule is that they are binding on the other cosharers, both in Bengal and under the Mitakshara. The manager is the agent for the other coparceners, with authority to do acts for their common necessity or benefit. The test of his authority is the degree in which he is held to be accountable by the Courts. Where there has been good faith, there is no right to an account by any coparcener to rectify past inequality of enjoyment. Such coparcener could at any time have claimed partition, and if he abstained from doing so he impliedly consented to what was expended. Special circumstances might give rise to such right to account, for instance, in Bengal, if the joint family carried on a joint business or an intention was shown that there should be such accountability (*a*). In all cases where a want of good faith was proved against a manager he would be obliged to account for his dealings. Where there is an ancestral trade, the infant members of the joint family will be bound by all acts of the manager necessary to the carrying on of the business, on the principle of a partnership amongst the members of the family including infants (*b*).

The nature of the account which may be directed on partition was explained by Mr. Justice Dwarkanath Mitter (*a*). The kurta, or other accountable member of the family, "is entitled to obtain credit from his coparceners for all sums of money bonâ fide spent by him for the benefit of the joint family, and he is certainly liable to make good to them their shares of all sums

(*a*) Obboychunder Roy Chowdhry *v.* Pearymohun Goopto, 5 Beng. L. R., 353; 13 Suth. W. R. F. B., 75.

(*b*) Ramlal Thakursidass *v.* Lakmichand Muniram, 1 Bomb. H. C. R. App., 51.

which he has actually misappropriated, or which he has spent for purposes other than those in which the joint family was interested. Of course, no member of a joint family is liable to his coparceners for anything which might have been actually consumed by him, in consequence of his having a larger family to support, or of his being subject to greater expenses than others: but this is simply because all such expenses are justly considered to be the legitimate expenses of the whole family. Thus, for instance, one member of a Hindu family may have a larger number of daughters to marry than the others. The marriage of each of these daughters is an obligation incumbent upon the whole family so long as it continues to be joint, and the expenses incurred by such marriage must necessarily be borne by all the members, without any reference whatever to their respective interests in the family estate." The principle on which such account is directed was defined by Chief Justice Couch as follows:—" The members of a joint Hindu family are entitled to the family property, subject to such dispositions of it as the managing member is entitled to make either by virtue of the power which is given to him by law as manager, or of the power which may be given to him by consent of the other members of the family. Subject to the exercise of these powers and to any disposition of any portion of the family property which may have been made by virtue of them, the other members of the family are clearly interested in that property." On the same principle English courts of equity act in the case of joint tenants and tenants in common.

As regards rights of maintenance whilst the estate continues joint: (1) Sons, grandsons, and great grandsons must all, under Mitakshara law, be maintained out of it. The right extends to every member of the family the man excluded from inheritance and the illegitimate offspring (*a*). In Bengal sons have not a legal right to maintenance from their father, for under the Bengal

(*a*) Mutuswamy Naiken *v.* V. Yettappa, 2 Beng. L. R. P.C., 15.

school he is absolute owner. Where the joint family consists of brothers, each is entitled to maintenance from the manager. (2) A wife of a coparcener is also entitled, unless she leave her husband's house; she does not forfeit her right if she leaves for just cause (*a*). A wife may recover maintenance from a purchaser of her husband's estate unless sold from necessity or without notice of her claim (*b*). (3) A widow's right to maintenance is a charge on the whole of her husband's estate; and in case of partition by her sons extends in Bengal to giving her a share equal to a son's; and under the Mitakshara also when the husband died separate from his brothers. The husband's relatives are not answerable for her maintenance, unless they have ancestral property in their hands (*c*). To protect a purchaser from her claim, he must have bought without notice of it or at a sale for necessity. A widow has also the right to live in her husband's family dwelling-house (*d*), and to leave it for just cause or without unchaste purpose (*e*). There is no general rule as to the amount of her maintenance. As against the joint family estate it will never exceed the share which her husband would have taken; the value of the estate, the amount of her own separate property, the expenses of living, and of her religious duties, even varying circumstances (*f*) will all be taken into consideration.

(4) A son's wife or widow is not entitled to maintenance from her father-in-law in Bengal (*g*); under the Mitakshara she is so out of the joint estate. At Bombay a son's widow was held entitled where there was no ancestral estate of her husband

(*a*) Lalla Gobind Pershad *v.* Dowlut Butee, 14 S. W. R., 451.

(*b*) Natchiar Ammal *v.* Gopala Krishna, Ind. L. R. 2 Mad., 127.

(*c*) Savitri Bai *v.* Luximi Bai, Ind. L. R. 2 Bomb., 573.

(*d*) Mangala Dabee *v.* Dinonath Bose, 4 Beng. L. R. O. C. J., 72.

(*e*) Raja Pirthi Singh *v.* Rani Raj Kowar, 20 Suth. W. R., 21.

(*f*) Rajendronath Raj *v.* Puttosoondry Dossee, 5 C. L. R., 18.

(*g*) Khettur Monee Dossee *v.* Kashee Nath Boso, 10 Suth. W. R. F. B., 89.

in her father-in-law's hauds; but later this doctrine was overruled (*a*). (5) Other female members, such as the mother and grandmother, are also entitled (*b*).

In order to make a claim of maintenance absolutely secure as against bonâ fide purchasers of the estate without notice, the way is to have the amount fixed by the court, and declared to be a charge on the estate. In general the widow is the only maintenance holder who can adopt this expedient.

The general rule with regard to a legal right to maintenance is that it depends upon whether there was any estate in respect of which it arises. As regards a right of maintenance founded only on relationship, the only persons who can claim are aged parents, wife, and minor children. But a Hindu can by his conduct bring himself under a legal obligation to maintain a dependent member of his family—for instance, the widow of a deceased son, where *primâ facie* the obligation would have been purely a moral one (*c*).

(*a*) Udaram Sitaram *v.* Sonka Bai, 10 Bomb. H. C. R., 483; cf. Kalu *v.* Kashi Bai, Ind. L. R. 7 Bomb., 130.

(*b*) Sheodyal Tewaree *v.* Jadoonath Tewaree, 9 S. W. R., 62.

(*c*) Khetramoni *v.* Kashinath, 2 B. L. R. A. C. J., 15.

CHAPTER III.

HINDU OWNERSHIP OR ESTATES.

Three classes of estates—Joint, separate, and woman's estate or stridhana—Joint as distinguished from ancestral estate—Impartible joint estate—Self-acquired estate—Effect of joint property being the nucleus of self-acquisition—Stridhana—Its special course of succession—Widow's estate—Her qualified proprietorship.

THERE are three classes of Hindu ownership or estates: (1) joint estate, (2) separate estate, (3) stridhana or woman's estate. Originally all property was joint; separate or self-acquired property was an exception of later origin. The class to which an estate belongs is determined by the mode of its acquisition.

Joint estate is usually acquired by inheritance and continued by survivorship; and in that case it is also called ancestral. When a joint family is owner of joint ancestral estate, it is vested in the coparceners, each of whom acquires his interest therein by birth, which varies in value according to the number of births and deaths of other coparceners, and passes by survivorship. It is inchoate and varying, completed by partition. On partition with collaterals a coparcener holds his share of ancestral estate joint with his own male issue; to separate from whom a further partition would be required. Savings out of ancestral estate, purchases out of its income, profits from the sale thereof are all joint ancestral estate; they follow the character of the fund, to which they are an increment. Ancestral estate, at all events immovable estate, cannot be so dealt with as between the members of the joint family as to lose the character of ancestral estate and to become self-acquired, either by deed of gift or will (*a*).

Not all joint estate is ancestral. Property jointly acquired is joint estate. It belongs to the joint acquirers (*b*). If those joint acquirers were members of a joint family and had made their acquisition with a nucleus of descended property, it would be ancestral as well as joint. Otherwise it would be joint as regards the acquirers, but self-acquired as regards both collaterals and lineals. If acquired by a single individual, his male issue would take no interest in it by birth; if acquired by several brothers, a similar result would follow (*c*). Another case of an estate being joint, but not ancestral, is where joint brethren succeed to the estate of a separated uncle. In that case they take by what is called obstructed inheritance—that is, their succession would have been obstructed by the birth of male issue to the separated uncle, and they took no interest in his estate by birth. Consequently it was not ancestral, although they succeeded to it jointly. Savings, profits, and purchases from or with joint funds follow the character of the fund from which they proceed. In Bengal there is little distinction between joint and ancestral estate, for there is in that school no inchoate interest by birth. Title accrues in that school at the death of the last owner.

Accordingly, though joint estate is usually ancestral, it is sometimes self-acquired: and on the other hand property though separately held may be joint, as, for instance, an impartible zemindari. Such impartible property is an exception to the usually partible character of joint estate. The separate holding of it cuts down the rights of enjoyment by the other members of the joint family to those of maintenance mainly.

(*a*) Muddun Gopal *v.* Ram Buksh Pandey, 6 S. W. R., 71, and Tara Chand *v.* Reeb Ram, 3 Mad. H. C., 50, 54.

(*b*) Compare Transfer of Property Act (IV. of 1882), s. 45.

(*c*) Chatturbhooj Meghji *v.* Dharamsi, Ind. L. R. 9 Bomb., 438.

But the mode of succession depends upon whether it is joint or self-acquired, as was decided in the Shivagunga case (*a*). Till lately it was considered that the power of alienation by the holder was as restricted as that of the holder of partible ancestral estate. It has been held that savings from an impartible estate are not an accretion to the impartible estate.

Separate estate usually results from partition. Self-acquired estate did not exist whilst the joint family system was in full vigour. The earliest forms of self-acquisition were the gains of science and valour to the Brahman and the Kshatriya. It came to include wealth acquired with a wife, gifts from relatives or friends, even ancestral property which had been lost and recovered by the independent exertion of a single member. A coparcener can self-acquire; and the test whether his acquisition is exclusively for himself or for the benefit of the joint family is whether it has been made without detriment to the joint estate. The joint estate must have been used for the immediate purpose of gain. Maintenance and education out of the joint funds are in general too remote, except where the training has been of a special character, with a view to subsequent reimbursement and profit for the joint benefit. The Madras and Bombay High Courts in past times ruled strongly in favour of joint and against separate acquisition (*b*). The High Court in Bengal and the Privy Council do not sanction the doctrine that early education from the joint funds incapacitates a man for self-acquisition (*c*).

It is for the self-acquirer to show, if he had possession of available joint funds, that his acquisition was made without detriment to them. If self-acquisition was made with borrowed

(*a*) 9 Moore, I. A., 539; s. c. 2 Suth. P.C., 31.

(*b*) Boologam *v.* Swornam, 4 Mad., 330. Durvasula Gungadharudu *v.* Narasammah, 7 Mad. H. C., 47. Bai Manchha *v.* Narotamdas, 6 Bomb. H. C. (A. C., J.), 1.

(*c*) Dhunookdaree *v.* Gunput Lall, 11 Beng. L. R., 201 note. Pauliem Valloo *v.* Pauliem Sooryah, L. R. 4 I. A., 109.

money, the joint credit must not have been pledged or the acquisition will be joint. And if the money has been borrowed from the family it must have been with a special agreement that the self-acquirer should have the sole risk and benefit.

Stridhana used to signify all kinds of property of which a woman has become the owner. Long usage has confined the term to that sort of property of which she has absolute control, excluding property which she has inherited from a male owner, and which is usually described as a widow's estate, even when inherited by a maiden daughter.

Menu (IX., sects. 194, 195) describes the sixfold separate property of a woman to include gifts at her marriage (called Yautaka) from her husband and her own family; gifts after marriage (called Ayautaka) from her husband and his family. According to the Dayabhaga (IV., 1, 15) a woman's stridhana consists of "her subsistence, her ornaments, her perquisites, and her gains." According to the Mitakshara (II., 11, 2) it consists of "property which she may have acquired by inheritance, purchase, partition, seizure, or finding." This text seems to include all the known methods of acquisition, and would in fact give the Hindu woman the absolute dominion over every kind of property which she possesses. It accordingly has not been acted upon, or recognised as any authority for the doctrine that all property which has devolved upon a woman by inheritance is her stridhana.

Stridhana usually denotes all the property of a woman "which she has power to give, sell, or use independently of her husband's control." But there is also a species of stridhana over which her control is limited by her husband, but by no one else; it is said to include immovable estate given to her by anyone, but especially if given by her husband.

Stridhana passes to a woman's heirs by a special course of succession; when once it has devolved upon an heir it ceases to be stridhana in the hands of the latter for all purposes including further descent (*a*), and descends from such heir according to the ordinary law.

All savings from and purchases with stridhana (*b*) and all arrears of maintenance (*c*) are stridhana.

There is an exception in Bombay to the rule that stridhana does not include property which a woman has inherited from a male owner. The High Court at Bombay holds that a woman takes absolutely the estate which she inherits from her father or brother. But it also holds that such stridhana descends to the woman's sons or other heirs in the same order of succession as if she had been a male; and not by the special order of succession usually applicable to stridhana.

That special order may be here stated. If the woman be unmarried her stridhana devolves at her death on her brothers, failing them it passes to her mother, next to her father, and failing him to the nearest relatives of her parents (*d*).

If the holder of stridhana be a married woman, there are different lines of succession, according to the nature and origin of the property. Her bridal gifts of movables go to her unmarried daughters first, and failing them to her married daughters, preference being given to the indigent. The dowry paid with her reverts to her parents who gave it; while gifts subsequent to her marriage are divided between her sons and daughters equally.

With regard to stridhana generally the main feature of the succession is the preference shown to the female line. The Benares order is: (1) the maiden daughter, (2) unmarried daughters, the indigent being preferred, (3) granddaughters, (4) daughters' sons and their issue *per stirpes*, (5) then her

(*a*) Prankissen *v.* Noyanmoney, I. L. R. 5, Calc 225. Compare Srinath Gangopadhya *v.* Sarbamangali Debi, 2 Beng. L. R. A. C., 144.

(*b*) Luchmun Chunder *v.* Kalli Churn, 19 S. W. R. P.C., 292.

(*c*) Court of Wards *v.* Mohessur Roy, 16 Suth. W. R., 76.

(*d*) Dayabhaga, b. IV., s. 3, vv. 6, 7.

husband and his heirs, if the marriage had been in the Brahma form; if not, to the parents, the mother taking precedence. The Bengal order of succession is regulated with more attention to funeral obsequies: (1) the unbetrothed daughters, (2) the betrothed, (3) the married, (4) the widowed or barren, (5) daughters who have or are likely to have sons. Grand-daughters are excluded, and sons precede daughters' sons. Failing lineal descendants, the husband or the parents succeed, according to the form of marriage which has been observed. If the stridhana were *ayautaka*—*i.e.*, not given at the time of marriage—it would be shared equally by sons and unmarried daughters.

With regard to stepdaughters, they and their issue have a place in the order of succession. The Mitakshara says that the stepdaughter in order to succeed must be sprung of a rival wife of a superior class to the deceased (*a*). The step-daughter's right has been recognised by judicial decision (*b*).

The other class of woman's estate, which is now treated as distinct from stridhana, is that which is known as widow's estate. This has always been difficult to define. In the absence of male issue the widow succeeds to all the estate to which the husband was separately entitled (whether or not partition had been completed by metes and bounds). "Of him," says Vrihaspati, "whose wife is not deceased, half the body survives" (*c*). Accordingly, her possession seems a sort of prolongation of her husband's possession; it terminates, of course, with her own life, and so is sometimes said to be a life estate. At her death it passes to her husband's heirs, ascertainable at her death. The succession to her husband opens at her death, as if her husband had lived on to that date. During the interval of her proprietorship she has rights in the estate,

(*a*) Mitakshara, c. II., s. 11, v. 22.

(*b*) Gosaien *v.* Kishenmunee, 6 Sel. rep. (Bengal), 77.

(*c*) Dayabhaga, c. XI., s. 1, v. 2.

and represents it in a way which requires to be strictly defined. Her widow's estate is defined by the Privy Council in the case of the Collector of Masulipatam *v.* Cavaly Vencata Narrainapah (*a*):—"It is clear that under the Hindu law the widow though she takes as heir takes a special and qualified estate. Compared with any estate that passes under the English law by inheritance, it is an anomalous estate. It is a qualified proprietorship, and it is only by the principles of the Hindu law that the extent and nature of the qualification can be determined." Those qualifications relate chiefly to the power of alienation, and to the extent to which under certain circumstances she represents, and can exercise the full ownership.

(*a*) 8 Moore, I. A., 550.

CHAPTER IV.

THE JOINT ESTATE.—POWER OF ALIENATION.—THE MANAGER.

Power of alienation according to the Bengal school—Of the coparcener—Of the manager or Kurta—According to the Mitakshara—Of the manager—Of the father—Right of the coparcener to dispute alienation—Limitations of the manager's authority—Restrictions on the father's power of alienation—Doctrines by which that power has been extended—Son's liability for his father's debts when not immoral—Hunoomanpershad Panday *v.* Mussamut Babooee—Gridharee Lall *v.* Kantoo Lall—Suraj Bunsi Koer *v.* Sheo Proshad Singh.

A SCHEME of aggregate ownership gives rise to a special law of alienation as well as to a special law of enjoyment. There is a broad difference between the systems of the Dayabhaga and Mitakshara in reference to the power of alienation.

Under the Bengal school the father is absolute owner, with an unfettered power of alienation. On his death, when his heirs jointly succeed, each co-heir has a separate right to an ascertained share, and has full power of alienation over his share, even while the property continues to be held by them in common as coparceners. The absolute disposing power of a Hindu father under the Bengal school was not established without considerable discussion. But in 1831 the judges of the Supreme and Sudder Courts in consultation declared that "a Hindu who has sons can sell, give, or pledge, without their consent, immovable, ancestral property situate in the province of Bengal; and that without their consent he can by will prevent, alter, or effect their succession to such property." (*a*) It is now clearly settled beyond all further question that the Hindu law, according to the school of Bengal, makes no distinction between ancestral or joint and self-acquired property as respects the right of alienation by sale, gift, will, or otherwise. To quote Lord Kingsdown: "Throughout Bengal a man who is the absolute owner of property may now dispose of it by will as he pleases, whether it be ancestral or not" (*b*). The rule may be stated even more broadly, viz., that he may dispose of his property, whether movable or immovable, ancestral or self-acquired, as he pleases by gift, sale, or will. The individual has in the Bengal school to a very great extent superseded the joint family as the owner of property, and his rights are absolute, whether over his self-acquired estate or his share of the joint estate. In no case does he require the concurrence of a co-owner in his alienation, nor is he impeded in any way, except when an ancestor's widow or other person has a charge on the estate in his hands sufficient to form an incumbrance thereon.

The law of this school, therefore, is the law of individual ownership, distinct from that of aggregate ownership under the Mitakshara. As a general rule, a coparcener under the Bengal school can only aliene his own share. The power of the manager to aliene the whole estate without the consent of other sharers who are capable of consenting can only arise in that school under most exceptional circumstances. Those circumstances must be such as would entitle him to act as their agent and representative, so that his alienation for their benefit would bind them on the ground of their implied consent. The power would arise more readily when the non-assenting coparcener is an infant, but its exercise would be carefully watched on the principle laid down by the Privy Council:

(*a*) Shamachwin's Vyavastha Darpana, p. 568.

(*b*) Nagalutchmee Ummal *v.* Gopoo Nadaraja Chetty, 6 Moore, I. A., 344.

"the power of a manager for an infant heir to charge an estate not his own is under the Hindu law a limited and qualified power. It can only be exercised rightly in a case of need or for the benefit of the estate. But where in the particular instance the charge is one that a prudent owner would make in order to benefit the estate, the bonâ fide lender is not affected by the precedent mismanagement of the estate. The actual pressure on the estate, the danger to be averted, or the benefit to be conferred upon it in the particular instance, is the thing to be regarded" (*a*).

Under the Mitakshara the power of alienation is entirely different. The coparcener has not a separate right to an ascertained share, but an undefined interest in the whole, varying as regards the amount of the share to which he will be entitled on partition, liable to be defeated altogether at his death before partition by his coparcener's rights of survivorship. Consequently his power to aliene is restricted. On the other hand, the power of the managing member to aliene the whole estate as compared with a managing coparcener under the Bengal system (not, of course, with the Bengal father, who is absolute proprietor) arises more readily under the Mitakshara system, since the consent of the coparceners who do not object will be more readily implied. The direct power of the manager to aliene is the same whether he is the father or the brother; in either case his power arises from his being the representative coparcener, and as such the agent of all the others, whose consent to his acts is either expressed or implied. But the indirect power of the father is much larger than that of any other manager, owing to the doctrine now fully established of his authority to bind his sons by contracting debts, so long as they are not tainted with immorality; and therefore to bind

(*a*) Hunooman Pershad Panday *v.* Musst Babooee Munraj Koonweree, 6 Moore, I. A., 393.

his sons by an alienation of joint estate to pay debts for which they, as well as himself, are answerable.

Except where the circumstances are such as to give to the manager the legal right to bind the other coparceners, he has no more power to aliene than any other coparcener. But it often happens that some of them are minors, or incapable of contracting, whether by reason of absence, minority, or any other disabling cause. Such incapacity on the part of some of the members confers powers of alienation in certain cases of necessity upon the managing owner, which he would not possess under ordinary circumstances or upon general principles of agency.

Not merely does this incapacity confer the power, but the existence of legal necessity by itself is sufficient for that purpose. A son who has attained the age of majority has no power to prevent his father's alienations of ancestral estate for the purpose of defraying joint debts or of providing for family maintenance. He can interdict acts of waste; but if he does not do so, and is cognisant of the transaction, and especially if he derives any benefit from it, he will be held to have impliedly assented to it. Justifying necessity is the usual ground on which alienation by a manager is supported; but the power in reality extends to all cases in which he is acting for the benefit of the family and of the joint estate, or as a prudent owner would act (*a*).

Where a brother or coparcener other than the father is the manager, the limitation on his authority arises from the joint character of the ownership in which all are interested. But where the father is the manager, there are several special considerations to be attended to. First, it is not yet finally settled whether he has not a special power of dealing with ancestral movable property for certain very special purposes. Second,

(*a*) Hunoomanpershad Panday *v.* Musst Babooee, 6 Moore, I. A., 393.

as regards his self-acquired property, the sons and others have no interest in it, nor in the share which comes to the father on partition with his sons. But a text in the Mitakshara (I., 1, 27) to the effect that a father "is subject to the control of his sons and the rest, in regard to the immovable estate, whether acquired by himself or inherited from his father or other predecessor," has given rise to a conflict of decision with regard to his absolute disposing power over self-acquired immovables. The High Courts at Madras (*a*) and Allahabad (*b*) have decided in the negative. The High Court at Calcutta has decided in the affirmative (*c*). It has also recently been held that a father may dispose of the joint family property free from the control of his coparceners if he holds it as impartible estate. Third, if the father has inherited his estate from a collateral relation, a brother, nephew, cousin, or uncle, or from an ancestor more remote than three degrees, or from or through a female, his sons cannot restrain his dealings with it. The reason is that in all those cases it was obstructed inheritance—that is, it might have been defeated, and he had no actual vested interest in it until the contingency happened, when it devolved upon him. Under such circumstances his sons acquire by birth no interest in it, and are not coparceners with him as in ancestral estate. Consequently they can neither restrain his alienation of it, nor compel him to come to a partition with them (*d*). Fourth, since the son's power to control his father's dispositions arises either from joint acquisition or from birth, he cannot object to any valid alienations made by his father before he was born or begotten. If at the time of such alienation there is no one living whose assent is necessary, or if those living have

(*a*) Tarachand *v.* Reeb Ram, 3 Mad. H. C., 55.

(*b*) Madasookh *v.* Budree, 1 N. W. P., 153 (1869).

(*c*) Mudden Gopal *v.* Ram Buksb, 6 Suth. W. R., 71, and see 12 Moore, I. A., 38.

(*d*) Nund Coomar Lall *v.* Razeeooddeen Hossein, 10 Beng. L. R., 183.

consented, the after-born son is bound by the transaction, whether a necessary one or not (*a*). If, on the other hand, it is so made that sons living at the time are not bound by it, neither will the after-born son be bound. Nor will any consent given by them after his birth avail; he can only be bound by their consent given before his birth (*b*).

Such are the main limitations to those co-existing rights of coparcener sons which usually operate to restrict the father's power. But there is another consideration which operates a wide extension of the father's powers, so wide as to bring the father's power of alienation under the Mitakshara law within measurable distance of the absolute power possessed by the father under the Bengal school. Over and above the power which he possesses in common with any other manager of joint family estate to aliene with consent express or implied from justifying necessity or on any other sufficient ground, he has the extensive power of alienation which results from the son's obligation to pay his debts out of ancestral estate, unless immoral. So far as the son is liable to pay his father's debts he is bound by the father's sale of ancestral estate to discharge such debts, even though they had been contracted without necessity or for any purpose whatever not recognised as immoral by the Hindu law.

This obligation, which the sons and grandsons share with the father, of paying his debts is a religious one, founded on the duty of discharging the debtor from sin. The obligation does not arise on the part of the son if his father's debt was such as not to create this moral obligation. Immoral debts are defined in Jagannatha's Digest: (*c*) "the sons are not compellable to pay sums due by their father for spirituous liquors, for losses at play, for promises made without any consideration,

(*a*) Girdharee Lall *v.* Kantoo Lall, L. R. 1 I. A., 321.

(*b*) Hurodoot *v.* Beer Narain, 11 S. W. R., 480.

(*c*) Dig. I., 5, 201-3, and see also 23 S. W. R., 260, and 25 S. W. R., 311.

or under the influence of lust or of wrath, or sums for which he was a surety (except in the cases before mentioned), or . . . any debt for a cause repugnant to good morals." The onus lies on the sons who claim exemption from this obligation to show that the specific debts for which the estate was sold were immoral, and this onus is not discharged by general evidence to the effect that the father was living an extravagant or immoral life when he contracted them (*a*).

This principle of liability was established by the Privy Council in the well-known case of Hunoomanpershad Panday *v.* Mt. Babooee (*b*), where Lord Justice Knight Bruce laid it down: "Unless the debt was of such a nature that it was not the duty of the son to pay it, the discharge of it, even though it affected ancestral estates, would still be an act of pious duty on the son. By the Hindu law the freedom of the son from the obligation to discharge the father's debt has reference to the nature of the debt, and not to the nature of the estate, whether ancestral or acquired by the creator of the debt." The son's obligation, therefore, is absolute; it has nothing to do with whether he or the estate derived any benefit from it, or with the character of the father's estate out of which it is payable; and it is not limited to the extent of the father's interest in that estate. The father's creditor therefore has, by virtue of the son's liability to pay his father's debts, an extensive remedy against the ancestral estate which operates to enlarge indefinitely the father's power of alienation. The leading case on this subject is that of Girdharee Lall *v.* Kantoo Lall (*c*); where a son sued to set aside (so far as his own share was concerned) his father's sale of ancestral estate to pay his own debts, on the ground that the sale was not with his consent, and that neither was the sale made, nor the debt contracted, for his benefit.

(*a*) Bhagbut Pershad *v.* Girja Koer, L. R. 15 I. A., 99.

(*b*) 6 Moore, I. A., 421.

(*c*) L. R. 1 I. A., 321.

The Privy Council examined the nature of the son's interest in the ancestral estate as to whether it extended to give him the right claimed. "Did he gain such an interest in this property as prevented it from being liable to pay a debt which his father had contracted? If his father had died and left him as his heir and the property had come into his hands, could he have said that because this was ancestral property which descended to his father from his grandfather it was not liable to pay his father's debts?" The answer given to that question is that the case in 6th Moore just cited established that ancestral property is not exempted from liability to pay the father's debts because a son is born to him. "If the debt of the father had been contracted for an immoral purpose, the son might not have been under any pious obligation to pay it; and he might possibly object to those estates which had come to the father as ancestral property being made liable to the debt. That was not the case here. It was not shown that the bond upon which the decree was obtained was given for an immoral purpose; it was a bond given apparently for an advance of money upon which an action was brought. The bond had been substantiated in a Court of Justice; there was nothing to show that it was given for an immoral purpose; and the holder recovered a decree upon it. There is no suggestion either that the bond, or the decree, was obtained benamee for the benefit of the father, or merely for the purpose of enabling the father to sell the family property and raise money for his own purpose. On the contrary, it was proved that the purchase money for the estate was paid into the bankers of the father, and credit was given to him with the bankers for that amount, and that the money was applied partly to pay off the decree, partly to pay off a balance which was due from the father to the bankers, and partly to pay Government revenue; and then there was some small portion of which the application was not accounted for. But it is not because a small portion is unaccounted for that the son has a right to turn out the bonâ fide purchaser who gave value for the estate and to recover possession of it with mesne profits. Even if there was no necessity to raise the whole purchase money, the sale would not be wholly void."

The effect of this decision is to enlarge the father's power of alienation so as to be co-extensive with his power to contract debts; and inasmuch as he is not subject to the control of his sons as regards the latter power, he is practically freed from their control as regards the former power. It created more surprise amongst Hindus than is easily accounted for. It is based upon an old well-established rule of Hindu law, which had been somewhat disregarded by the Courts in India, that it is the pious duty of a Hindu son to pay his father's debts. It tended to abolish the fraudulent practices which had become rife in Mitakshara districts of putting forward the sons to contest creditors' claims created by the father. Yet it did not pass without hostile comment, especially in Madras, where the joint family system has been specially protected and encouraged One of the judges of the Madras High Court went so far as to say, "The decision of the Privy Council is contrary to what is understood to be the Hindu law in the Madras Presidency as established by a long series of decisions which the Judicial Committee, in arriving at their conclusion, did not notice. I think we are not bound by the novel view taken by the Judicial Committee in this respect" (*a*). The son was always liable to pay his father's debts out of his father's estate; but that liability was founded on his taking the assets of his father by inheritance, and his liability was always limited to the amount of those assets. In Bombay, however, previous to Bombay Act VII. of 1866 a Hindu was held liable to pay his father's debts with interest, and his grandfather's debts without interest, regardless of whether he had inherited assets or

(*a*) Ponnappa Pillai *v.* Pappuvayyangar, I. L. R. 4 Mad., 14.

not (*a*). The Act mentioned was passed to prescribe a more equitable rule. The rule laid down in Girdharee Lall *v.* Kantoo Lall applies to ancestral estate; where the son would take his father's estate by survivorship by a title paramount to that of the creditor, but for the rule there enforced that he and therefore all that he takes by survivorship is liable to pay the father's debts. So far from its being a novel view, Lord Justice Knight Bruce in the case of Hunoomanpershad Panday *v.* Mt. Baboolall Munraj Koonweree (*b*) laid down that "though an estate be ancestral, it may be charged for some purposes against the heir for the father's debt by the father. . . . Unless the debt was of such a nature that it was not the duty of the son to pay it, the discharge of it, even though it affected ancestral estate, would still be an act of pious duty in the son. By the Hindu law the freedom of the son from the obligation to discharge his father's debt has respect to the nature of the debt and not to the nature of the estate, whether ancestral or acquired by the creator of the debt." Possibly the effect of this ruling was for a time imperfectly appreciated by some of the Courts in India. The logical result, however, was that in Girdharee Lall *v.* Kantoo Lall (*c*) it was held that as the father's debts were not immoral, the son could not set aside his father's sale of ancestral estate in order to satisfy them; for he as well as his father was liable to pay them, at least so far as the ancestral estate extended. In Suraj Bunsi Koer *v.* Sheo Proshad Singh (*d*) the sons proved that by reason of the nature of the father's debts, neither they nor their interests in the joint ancestral estate were liable to satisfy their father's debt; and accordingly all that remained to be decided was whether the father's coparcenary share passed

(*a*) Narasimbharav *v.* Antaji, 2 Bomb. H. C., 61, 65.

(*b*) 6 Moore, I. A., 421.

(*c*) L. R. 1 I. A., 321.

(*d*) L. R. 6 I. A., 88, 108.

to the purchaser at the execution sale, which turned upon the question whether the execution creditors had gone far enough to establish a valid charge thereon before the debtor's death. It was held that they had, since the creditor had obtained a decree, an attachment, and an order for sale during the lifetime of his debtor, although the actual sale did not take place till after his death.

CHAPTER V.

THE JOINT ESTATE.—POWER OF ALIENATION.—THE COPARCENER.

Power of coparcener to aliene under the Mitakshara—Voluntary alienations—Doctrine of the Bengal High Court—In the North-West—In Madras and Bombay—Practical result of the conflicting decisions—Alienations under execution sales against a coparcener—Remedies of a judgment creditor against a coparcener's right, title, and interest—Deendyal *v.* Jugdeep Narain Singh—Suraj Bunsi Koer *v.* Sheo Proshad.

WE pass from the powers under the Mitakshara law of the father or other manager respectively to alienate the whole ancestral estate to the question under the same law as to the right of each coparcener to aliene his coparcenary interest—that is, the share to which in the event of partition he would be entitled. The difficulty arises from this, that his interest in the estate ceases with his life, and passes at his death to the surviving coparceners. The further difficulty arises as to the relations which will exist between the purchaser of his coparcenary interest and the rest of the coparceners.

The subject divides itself into two heads: (1) voluntary alienations by a coparcener ; (2) compulsory alienations under execution sales of a coparcener's interest.

With regard to voluntary alienations by a coparcener of his interest—that is, the share to which he would be entitled on partition—it was decided broadly in Sadabart Prasad Sahu *v.* Foolbash Koer (*a*) by a Full Bench of the High Court of Bengal that "no cosharer before partition can, without the

(*a*) 3 Beng. L. R. F. B., 39.

assent of all the cosharers, determine the joint character of the property by conveying away his share." There had been conflicting decisions on the subject, but the Full Bench ruled that although one member of a joint family under that law can compel a partition against the will of his coparceners, yet he had no authority to mortgage his undivided share. Authorities both ancient and recent were cited in favour of that view, which has since been approved by the Privy Council (*a*); and it was pointed out that if he could do so, he would thereby prejudice the rights of those who might afterwards be born, and who would at birth be entitled to share in the estate, including the portion conveyed away by the coparcener. Although the whole family may, regardless of the interests of unborn descendants, aliene the whole estate, each coparcener has not the same power over a share which, until partition has definitely ascertained it, is of variable extent, according as it is affected by subsequent births and deaths in the family.

This Bengal decision is in confirmation of a series of decisions in the North-West Provinces; and the Privy Council case just cited recognises it as settled law in both divisions of the Bengal Presidency that a Hindu cannot, without the consent of his coparceners, sell or mortgage his undivided share in the ancestral estate for his own benefit. The Courts of those two divisions of the same Presidency had decided against the coparcener's interest passing, either by voluntary alienation or under an execution sale. The validity of the alienation by execution sale was left open by the Full Bench in Foolbash Kooer's case, but has since been upheld by the Privy Council.

In Madras and Bombay the earlier decisions were adverse to the coparcener's power of aliening his undivided share. In Madras that was the rule down to 1860. But subsequently to that a change took place (*b*), and the High Court ruled in favour

(*a*) Balgobind Das *v.* Narain Lal, L. R. 20 I. A., 116.

(*b*) Virasvami *v.* Ayyasvami, 1 Mad. H. C., 471.

of a coparcener's undivided share passing, whether by a voluntary alienation or by an execution sale, in a judgment which decides that "what the purchaser or execution creditor of the coparcener is entitled to is the share to which, if a partition took place, the coparcener himself would be individually entitled, the amount of such share of course depending upon the state of the family." That decision has been repeatedly followed and settles the law in the Madras Presidency. In Bombay the earlier decisions, which were to the same effect as the earlier decisions in Madras, were departed from earlier than in Madras; for both the Bombay Sudder and Supreme Courts acquiesced eventually in the doctrine that a purchaser of a coparcener's interest could maintain a suit for partition, and thus obtain the share which he had purchased. In Vasudev *v.* Venkatesh (*a*) an elaborate judgment declared that "it must be regarded as the settled law of this Presidency, not only that one of several coparceners in a Hindu family may, before partition, and without the assent of his coparceners, sell, mortgage, or otherwise aliene for valuable consideration his share in the undivided family estate, movable or immovable, but also that such share may be taken in execution under a judgment against him at the suit of his personal creditor."

There are two limitations to the rule thus laid down in Madras and Bombay in opposition to that which obtains through the entire Presidency of Bengal, viz., that both in Madras (*b*) and Bombay (*c*) a coparcener may not aliene his divided share by will or gift. A purchaser for value is entitled where a volunteer is not.

These limitations show that the Courts in Madras and Bombay, though they have established that a coparcener may

(*a*) 10 Bomb. H. C., 139, 160, followed by Full Bench decision, *ibid.*, 162.

(*b*) Vitla Butten *v.* Yamenamma, 8 Mad. H. C., 6.

(*c*) Vrandavandas *v.* Yamunabai, 12 Bomb. H. C., 229: Ramanna *v.* Venkata, I. L. R. 11 Mad. 246: and see on this subject Lakshman *v.* Ramchandra, L. R. 7 I. A., 195.

aliene his share, are not disposed to carry that principle further than the previous course of decisions compelled them. And where alienation is allowed the coparcener cannot sell a specific share, but merely his undivided and unascertained interest in the whole, to be worked out by the process of partition and account.

It must be remembered that the interest so to be worked out is variable; that the extent of it depends upon the date fixed for ascertaining it; and if the coparcener who has aliened dies before his interest is ascertained and vested in his alienee, there is the conflicting right by survivorship on the part of his coparceners. The exact nature of the purchaser's rights and remedies has not yet been judicially ascertained. It is probable that a purchaser who has not completed the transaction, or who has not advanced far enough towards completion, will find that his rights by purchase are defeated by the coparcener's paramount rights by survivorship. That the extent of his interest would depend not upon the state of the family at the date of his purchase, but upon the state of the family at the date when he proceeded to enforce it has been recently decided by the High Court at Madras (*a*).

While the High Courts at Calcutta and Allahabad, on the one hand, are at variance from the High Courts at Madras and Bombay, on the other, as to the power of the coparcener to aliene his share or interest, the practical result is generally very similar. For in Bombay and Madras the purchaser works out his remedies by stepping into his vendor's shoes and himself compelling as a coparcener his remedies by partition and account. In Bengal he does not acquire the right to enforce as purchaser the rights of his vendor, for he took no title by his purchase. But the Bengal High Court has held that although a purchaser does not acquire title by reason of his vendor's inability to convey whilst his share is unascertained

(*a*) Rangasami *v.* Krishnayyan, I. L. R. 14 Mad., 408.

and undivided, he does acquire an equity to compel his vendor himself to proceed to partition. That is, although the High Court is bound to set aside the sale as inoperative, it will only do so on terms. And the terms insisted upon in one case (*a*) were that a partition should be at once effected, and that the shares of the coparceners who had aliened by way of mortgage should be held subject to a charge in favour of the mortgagor.

If this ruling is eventually upheld by the Privy Council the result will differ very little from that which is established in Madras and Bombay. In Madras and Bombay, however, the purchaser has a well-defined legal right. In Bengal he has only an equitable right dependent on the discretion of the Court in the particular case; which right, if recognised, may possibly be more readily defeated by the death of the vendor or his disability to sue for partition.

So far with regard to voluntary alienations. There is however the other division of the subject, which relates to the right of a creditor of one coparcener to seize and sell in execution of a decree that coparcener's right, title and interest in his ancestral estate. The principle in such a case is that a coparcener's debts are a charge on his coparcenary interest, but not a first charge so as to bind the interest. On the contrary, if the coparcener dies, the survivors will take by a paramount title, and the creditor's claims will be defeated, unless he has taken such steps as to gain for himself the preferential title so as to defeat the claims by survivorship. Where the debtor was father to the other coparceners, the creditor's right would prevail, by reason of the sons' liability to pay their father's debts when not immoral. Where the debtor is not a father, but on an equal footing with the other coparceners, the creditor's right and remedy against him and against his coparceners' rights by survivorship require elucidation.

(*a*) Mahabeer Persad *v.* Ramyad Singh, 12 Beng. L. R., 90.

The case of Deendyal *v.* Jugdeep Narain (*a*), decided by the Privy Council in 1877, establishes this rule, that where the creditor of a coparcener has obtained a decree against him in respect of his separate debt, he may enforce it *during his debtor's lifetime* by seizure and sale of his coparcenary interest. This conclusion was arrived at after an elaborate examination of the authorities; and it seems clear that a desire to enforce the creditor's rights first led in Madras and Bombay to breaking in upon the rule which rendered a coparcener's share inalienable without the consent of his coparceners. And having once established that a creditor could compel its alienation, the coparcener's power to aliene it voluntarily naturally followed. In Bengal the right of an execution creditor was not so readily admitted as in the other Presidencies. But the sanctity which Hindu law ascribes to a debt has ultimately prevailed, so that the liability of the whole estate for the father's debts, and the liability of the coparcener's interest to satisfy the coparcener's debts have become established principles.

Deendyal's case, however, stopped short at this, that the judgment creditor could seize and sell in execution during his debtor's lifetime, leaving the question open whether on his debtor's death before seizure and sale the surviving coparceners could defeat the judgment creditor's rights. The purchaser, however, at such sale could not claim any specific share of the ancestral estate as his debtor's property; he could only proceed by partition, exercising in relation thereto the rights which his debtor had possessed.

It will be seen on reference to the reported case that the judgment was directed to this issue, "whether under the law of the Mitakshara the share of one cosharer in a joint family estate can be taken and sold in execution of a decree against

(*a*) L. R. 4 I. A., 247.

him alone." It is quite clear that by the Hindu law of the Bengal school it can. The High Courts of Madras and Bombay, it was pointed out, had ruled that it could even under the Mitakshara. And the Full Bench of the High Court in Bengal, in the case of Sadabart *v.* Phoolbash Koer had left the point undecided, although they held, contrary to the rulings in the other Presidencies, that a cosharer could not himself aliene his share. At the same time, by a later decision in 1872, the High Court in Bengal had held that the purchaser of such share at an execution sale acquired a lien on it. Their Lordships, upon this state of the authorities, remarked, "there appears to be little substantial distinction between the law thus enunciated (*i.e.*, by the decision of 1872) and that which has been established in Madras and Bombay, except that the application of the former may depend upon the view which the judges may take of the equities of the particular case: whereas the latter establishes a broad and general rule defining the right of the creditor."

The Privy Council assuming, as in a much later case they decided, that voluntary alienations by a coparcener of his share were illegal by the Mitakshara, as understood in Bengal, proceeded as follows:—"However nice the distinction between the rights of a purchaser under a voluntary conveyance and those of a purchaser under an execution sale may be, it is clear that a distinction may, and in some cases does, exist between them. It is sufficient to instance the seizure and sale of a share in a trading partnership at the suit of a separate creditor of one of the partners. The partner could not himself have sold his share so as to introduce a stranger into the firm without the consent of his copartners, but the purchaser at the execution sale acquires the interest sold, with the right to have the partnership accounts taken in order to ascertain and realise its value. It seems to their Lordships that the same principle may and ought to be applied to shares in a joint and undivided

Hindu estate, and that it may be so applied without unduly interfering with the peculiar status and rights of the coparceners in such an estate, if the right of the purchaser at the execution sale be limited to that of compelling the partition which his debtor might have compelled had he been so minded, before the alienation of his share took place."

The foundation of this decision is that the judgment creditor had acquired against the coparcener, by virtue of his debt, decree, attachment, and sale, a valid charge upon the land to the extent of the coparcener's share. If the charge had not been created, and the creditor had merely an ordinary claim, his remedy would have disappeared with the death of his debtor, for at that moment his share would have passed to his surviving coparceners, and would no longer have been answerable for the debts of the deceased.

Deendyal's case, in which the creditor's seizure and sale took place during the debtor's lifetime, was followed by that of Suraj Bunsi Koer *v.* Sheo Proshad (*a*), in which the sale took place after the debtor's death, in pursuance of a judgment, attachment, and order for sale obtained during his life. The coparcener in that case was a father whose liability was in respect of immoral debts, from which the sons were free, so that it did not differ from the case of an ordinary coparcener. The Privy Council held that, although the actual sale had not taken place during the debtor's lifetime, still the execution proceedings had proceeded so far as to constitute in favour of the judgment creditor a valid charge upon the land to the extent of his debtor's share and interest therein. They further held that that charge could not be defeated by the debtor's death before actual sale. The seizable character of a coparcener's interest was established by Deendyal's case. That being so, the execution sale transferred the interest which had belonged

(*a*) L. R. 6 I. A., 88.

to the coparcener during his life, and the creditor was held to be entitled, notwithstanding the debtor's death and the claims of his surviving coparceners, to work out the rights which he had acquired under the execution proceedings by means of a partition.

CHAPTER VI.

The Joint Estate.—Partition.

Partition according to the Mitakshara—Period of partition—According to the Dayabhaga—Status of parcenership—Determined by partition and otherwise—How partition is effected—Property exempt from partition—Estates indivisible from their nature—Raj—Polliam—Ghatwali lands—Service tenures.

Partition is an important branch of the Hindu law, since under the Mitakshara system it is a recognised source of proprietary right. It applies to all property which is held as joint property in coparcenary, excluding therefore self-acquisitions and property which, though joint in character, is by custom impartible. Partition (*vibhaga*), according to the Mitakshara, is the adjustment of divers rights regarding the whole joint estate by distributing them over particular portions of it; and, on the other hand, reunion is the divesting of exclusive rights in these particular portions and re-vesting a common right over the whole. That treatise contemplates a division or reunion of title, while the Dayabhaga treats the title as always divided, and regards the thing which is the subject of property as alone divisible by the act of the parties. Under the Dayabhaga partition is an affair of metes and bounds, and is usually called a buttwara.

There are theoretically three periods of partition according to the Mitakshara: the first being at the option of the father; the second at the option of the sons in his lifetime, if there be no prospect of further issue, either on account of the father's age or on account of the age of both parents; thirdly, which is the most usual period for it to take place, after the decease of the father.

According to the Dayabhaga, the power of the sons to partition only arises on the extinction of the father's ownership. There are therefore only two periods of partition recognised by that treatise: one, when the father's property having ceased each son can demand partition; the other, when the father still retaining the proprietary right nevertheless chooses to divide his property amongst his sons. As he is absolutely entitled, it is now the established law that he may divide it as he pleases, the legal power of alienation being entirely unfettered in its exercise by the moral prohibitions, which are so frequently reiterated. It is further insisted in the Dayabhaga that the sons should not partition the ancestral estate until after the death of both parents; for as Vyasa says:—"For brethren a common abode is ordained, so long as both parents live; but after their decease religious merits of separated brethren increase" (*a*). But this rule is not observed in practice; the mother, however, on a partition by her sons, taking a share equal to that of a son, but having no right herself to call for a division of the estate.

Partition therefore must be chiefly studied as a part of the Mitakshara system. Until it is effected the descendants of a common ancestor are possessed of the rights and obligations which grow out of the *status* of an undivided family. Their exclusion from those rights is not necessarily governed by the same law which regulates their exclusion from inheritance. Heirship is governed by the law of the ancestor without regard to the law of the heir; but parcenership must be dealt with in reference to the law of the parcener. For instance, a Hindu who is an outcast, or who has renounced the Hindu religion, or who has become a convert to Christianity, whatever may be

(*a*) Dayabhaga, Chap. III., sec. 1, verse 8.

his rights of inheritance, having regard to the operation of Act XXI. of 1850, and the Regulations which deal with that subject, is at once severed from the Hindu family and deprived of his right to retain the *status* of coparcenership. The tie (*a*) which binds the family together is, so far as he is concerned, not only loosened, but dissolved. The obligation consequent upon and connected with the tie must be dissolved with it. Parcenership is put an end to by a severance effected by partition; it must equally be put an end to by a severance which the Hindu law recognises and creates.

Such was the doctrine of the Privy Council in the celebrated case of Abraham *v.* Abraham (*a*). The *status* of parcenership which devolves under the Mitakshara on a Hindu at birth, and is created by operation of law, considerably influences while it continues his rights and duties, and determines the rules of succession by which his property is effected. Such legal *status* is wholly different from that which is effected by agreement of parties to live or hold property jointly. It is at once determined by the happening of an event which, like that of conversion of one or more of the parceners, is legally inconsistent with its continuance, and operates to sever the relationship in person and property which law originally imposed.

This status of coparcenership is put an end to by the division of the title without waiting for the actual partition by metes and bounds and the allotment of the divided shares of the property to the parceners. Division is a word of two-fold application. There may be a division of title and there may be a division of the subject to which the title applies. Where a deed of partition had been executed the Privy Council held that that amounted to a division of right, even though it was not intended to be followed up by an actual partition by metes and bounds. Such a deed operated as a division of right, and

(*a*) Abraham *v.* Abraham, 9 Moore, I. A., 195.

therefore as a conversion of the character of the property and an alteration of the title of the family, converting it from a joint to a separate ownership (*a*). But where partition is effected by agreement, it must be clearly shown that the title was intended to be divided, and the enjoyment intended to be separate. The best proof of such agreement is that it has been followed up by actual division and allotment; but the separate appropriation of profits is sufficiently effective (*b*) for the purpose. The shares must be defined, and the agreement acted upon in such a way as to show that it is intended forthwith to carry it into operation. Separation from commensality does not effect partition, and is probably not sufficient evidence by itself of an intention to carry into effect an agreement to divide title (*c*).

The class of property which is exempt from partition includes all self-acquired estate both movable and immovable, so long as it was acquired without detriment to the joint estate. It includes also property which has been inherited by a single person, either collaterally, or by or through a female, or from a male ancestor more than three degrees remote; in such property his issue could claim no inchoate right by birth, and therefore no claim to partition. It includes also property already allotted to a man on a previous partition only to this extent that it is no longer partible while in his hands except as between himself and his own descendants, and not even with them if the previous partition had effected a severance from them. Things indivisible from their very nature are also excluded from partition, such as clothes and other subjects of special appropriation. Places of worship and sacrifice are also impartible (*d*). To divide buildings used for those purposes would

(*a*) Appoovier *v.* Rama Subba Ayan, 8 Suth. W. R. P.C., 1.
(*b*) Cheytnarain Singh *v.* Bunwaree Singh, 23 S. W. R., 397.
(*c*) Rewun Pershad *v.* Radha Beeby, 7 S. W. R. P.C., 35, 37.
(*d*) Anundmoyee Chowdhrain *v.* Boykantnath Roy, 8 S. W. R., 193.

be to render them utterly unsuited for the purposes and objects for which they are intended. Such buildings are always left joint, when a partition is made by a Collector under the provisions of Regulation XIX. of 1814. Parties jointly entitled to the use of such buildings "can enjoy their turn of worship, unless they can agree to a joint worship, and any infringement of the right to a turn in the worship can be redressed by a suit." "We cannot," said the High Court of Bengal, "permit the object for which they were erected to be neutralised by dividing them." Dewutter lands also are impartible. Those for whose benefit they are dedicated can by consent form separate religious establishments, and assign to each a *palla* or turn of worship. In Madras however it is different. There a single member of the family usually obtains the management, and is called the Dhamakarta, his office being regarded as impartible and held for life (*a*).

Then there are properties which are regarded as in their nature or on the ground of long usage impartible. To this class belong principalities and extensive zemindaries in the case of great families, where the usage is proved.

With respect to a raj as a principality, the general rule is that it is impartible (*b*). It is a sovereignty, a principality, subordinate no doubt, but still a limited sovereignty and principality, which in its very nature excludes the idea of division amongst the sons.

In the case of Baboo Teluckdharee Sahie *v.* Maharajah Rajendur Protab Sahie (*c*), the High Court of Bengal said "we do not find that it is anywhere definitely laid down what a raj is. There are many decisions in which estates have been found to be raj, or principalities, but what exactly

(*a*) Manally Chenna *v.* Mangadu Vaidelinga, I. L. R. 1 Mad., 346.

(*b*) Baboo Gunesh Dutt Singh *v.* Maharaja Moheshur Singh, 6 Moore, I. A., 187.

(*c*) Sutherland's F. B. Rulings, p. 97.

constitutes a raj has not, so far as we are aware, been anywhere set forth." One of the judges defined it to be "a principality which by universal custom must be preserved entire. The succession must be single, and whatever family usage governs it must continue to prevail. Upon a permanent breach of any of these particulars, the raj would become extinct." The Court added: "We will not go the length of saying that under no circumstances can property which constitutes a raj be divided, for it may pass into the hands of strangers, say in right of purchase at public auction for arrears of Government revenue, and it is impossible to hold that the purchaser, whoever he may be, has no power of making any disposition of the property, but that his first-born son has, in right of birth, an indefeasible title to the whole and entire estate. We do think, however, that while the estate remains in the same family, having come down from father to son or to some other single member, the rule of impartibility must prevail."

Again, a Polliam is a tract of country subject to a petty chieftain. It is in the nature of a raj. It may belong to an undivided family, but it is not the subject of partition. It can be held by only one member of the family at a time, who is styled the Polligar, the other members of the family being entitled to a maintenance or allowance out of the estate.

Ghatwali and other service tenures are usually impartible: so also estates granted as in Oudh by the Government in the exercise of sovereign power.

CHAPTER VII.

THE JOINT ESTATE.—PARTITION.

The right to call for a partition—Under the Dayabhaga—Under the Mitakshara—Right of sons, grandsons, great-grandsons—After-born sons—Minors—Agreement in restraint of partition—Persons disqualified to take on partition—Illegitimate sons—Equality of partition—Rights of widows—Of wives—Effect of partition.

THE next branch of the law of partition relates to the right to call for or put in motion the machinery by which a partition is effected. This again must be treated of with respect to the rival doctrines of the Mitakshara and the Dayabhaga, for according to the former every male member of the family is a coparcener with all the rights of a co-proprietor ; whereas in the latter the father's power completely overwhelms and destroys whatever rights may theoretically pertain to the son.

Amongst brethren, according to the Dayabhaga, each one or his representatives have a right to insist upon a partition. A mother cannot demand a partition as against her sons, but a widow can demand it as against her deceased husband's brothers. The co-proprietorship under this school is very similar to the tenancy in common in English law; the tenancy is severed, and the right to call for such severance is regulated upon very similar principles to those which are laid down in English law.

As regards the Mitakshara, to quote the High Court at Calcutta (*a*), "it is a settled doctrine of the Hindu law that every member of a joint undivided family has an indefeasible

(*a*) Musst Deo Bunsee Kooer *v.* Dwarkanath, 10 S. W. R., 273, 274.

right to demand partition of his own share. The other members of the family must submit to it whether they like it or not. According to the Mitakshara, a son is competent to compel even his own father to divide the family estate when that estate is joint and ancestral."

The High Courts of Bengal, Madras, North-West Provinces, and Bombay have all of them decided that a son or a grandson can claim partition of both movable and immovable property in the possession of a father against his consent (*a*); and that has been recognised as the settled law, as far as regards immovables, by the Privy Council in Suraj Bunsi *v.* Sheo Pershad (*b*). The great grandson would stand on the same footing; but it must be remembered that the right of any descendant to call for a partition assumes that his immediate ancestor is dead (*c*). A grandson cannot claim while his father is living, but as soon as his father dies he has by right of representation the same claim to a partition as against his grandfather and all other co-parceners which his father had. While his father was alive his father had the right to a share on partition, in which share when allotted his sons would be joint with him, and in their turn could compel him to partition. But they cannot compel him to call for a partition, and until he has done so their own rights to shares have not accrued, although they have a vested inchoate interest in the joint estate.

With regard to after-born sons the rule seems to be that if the pregnancy be known, the partition should be deferred till it is ascertained whether the child is a son, and therefore entitled to share. Otherwise a redistribution of shares must take place in his interest. Other views are (*d*) that he will

(*a*) Laljeet *v.* Rajcoomar, 12 B. L. R., 373. Nagalinga *v.* Subbiramaniya I. L. R. 1 Mad., 77.

(*b*) L. R. 6 I. A., 105.

(*c*) Rai Bishenchand *v.* Asmaida L. R. 11 I. A. 179 Apaji Narbar *v.* Ramchandra I. L. R. 16 Bomb. F. B. 29, but see Jogul Kishore *v.* Shib Sahai J. L. R. 5 All. 430.

(*d*) Kalidas *v.* Krishan Chandra, 2 B. L. R. F. B., 118.

take the father's share to the exclusion of his brothers, or that if the father has not retained one, the sons must allot him a share from their own. The after-born son must have been begotten before partition, for proprietary right begins with conception (*a*). Partition can take place notwithstanding the minority of some of the coparceners (*b*).

A minor however cannot enforce partition merely at his own option or at the option of his guardian; there must be reasonable ground for his insisting upon it. The Madras High Court declared that the true rule (*c*) to be observed was that a suit on behalf of a minor for partition would lie if the interests of the minor were likely to be prejudiced by the property being left in the hands of the coparceners from whom it is sought to recover it.

An agreement whereby the coparceners consent with one another that the property shall remain joint, and that the right to partition shall not be exercised, will only bind those who enter into it. It is not a consent which will run with each coparcenary right, into whose soever hands it may pass. Where a purchaser at a sheriff's sale of a share of an estate belonging to a Hindu joint family sued for partition, it was held that he was not bound by an agreement amongst the members not to partition (*d*).

Persons disqualified from inheriting are also disqualified from receiving shares on a partition. His next heir, if he would be entitled on the death of the disqualified person, will take instead of him. If the disqualification arises subsequent to partition, it does not work a forfeiture of the allotted share; if it is removed subsequent to partition, his right to a share is similar to that of a son born after partition.

(*a*) Yekeyamian *v.* Agniswarian, 4 Mad. H. C., 307.
(*b*) Musst Deo Bunsee Kooer *v.* Dwarkanath, 10 Suth. W. R., 273.
(*c*) Kamakshi Ammal *v.* Chidambara Reddi, 3 Mad. H. C., A. J., 94.
(*d*) Anandchandra Ghose *v.* Prankisto Dutt, 3 B. L. R., O. C., 14.

Illegitimate sons of the three higher castes are not entitled to shares. Amongst Sudras it seems that they are as against their brothers, but not as against their fathers (*a*). At a partition equality of division amongst the coparceners is the almost universal rule; the few exceptions to it having fallen into general disuse.

The rights of the female members of the family give rise to some differences. The only instance of a woman being a coparcener is that of a sonless widow in Bengal, where the husband died joint with his brethren. She succeeds to his share, and on partition it must be allotted to her; and she can if she chooses sue for partition (*b*). If there are sons she cannot claim partition against them, being only entitled to maintenance until division; but if they partition they must allot to her a share equal to each of theirs. If she is only stepmother to such sons she is not entitled to a share, but only to maintenance. Where there are two widows both having male issue, each mother is entitled to share with her own sons; if either widow has an only son, she does not share with him, but her right to maintenance is a charge on his share, not on the whole estate (*c*). If the only son dies, and the grandsons partition, the grandmother will be entitled to share with them.

Where there are several widows and no male issue the widows take by a joint title, and the survivor will take the whole. They can partition, but if they do they can only divide the enjoyment not the title, which remains that of the deceased husband, descendible to his heirs on the death of the survivor (*d*).

Wives are not under any circumstances, or according to any of the schools, allowed to demand a partition. But if the

(*a*) Sadu *v.* Baiza, I. L. R. 4 Bomb., 37, 44. Thangam Pillai *v.* Suppa Pillai, I. L. R. 12 Mad., 401.

(*b*) Dhurm Das Pandey *v.* Shama Soondri, 3 Moore, I. A., 229.

(*c*) Hemangini Dasi *v.* Kedarnath, L. R. 16 I. A., 115.

(*d*) Bhugwandeen *v.* Myna Baee, 11 Moore, I. A., 487.

father partitions, he must reserve to his wife a share for her maintenance in addition to the share which he takes himself (*a*). It is held in Madras, founding on the Smriti Chandrika, which is of authority there, that the right of a widow to a share is in lieu of maintenance. Consequently, though her share can never exceed that of a son, it is liable to be diminished, at all events in that Presidency, if the share would be greater than she needs for that purpose, or if she be already in possession of separate property (*b*). But this rule does not hold good elsewhere, except possibly in Bombay.

With regard to the legal effect of the act of partition, it may be said in general terms that according to the Bengal School it terminates the joint enjoyment of the parties, and according to the Mitakshara it puts an end to the joint ownership together with the rights of survivorship which flow from it, with respect to the estate to which the joint ownership applied. But there is (*c*) no principle of law on which it can be held that a Hindu, under Mitakshara law, acquires by partition with his brothers a greater dominion as against his sons over the share which he took under it than he previously had over the whole of the property. The share so taken is still property which has descended to him from his father, ancestral, not self-acquired. The adjustment of the rights over it cannot be held to amount to a new or self-acquisition by each allottee. Divided shares follow the same course of descent as self-acquired property. But they are distinguishable in this, that there is not the same power of alienation in the case of a separate share of ancestral estate as there is in the case of self-acquired property. Partition also, as we shall see, affects rights of inheritance according to the Benares School, in particular a widow's right of succession

(*a*) Lalljeet Sing *v.* Rajcumar Sing, 20 S. W. R., 336. Judoonath *v.* Bishonath, 9 Suth. W. R., 61. Krishori *v.* Moni Mohun, I. L. R. 12 Cal., 165.

(*b*) Venkatammal *v.* Andyappa, L. R. 6 Mad., 130; 8 Mad., 107, 123.

(*c*) See Lakshmibai *v.* Ganpat Moroba, 5 Bombay H. C. R., O. C. J., 128.

to her sonless husband, which only accrues where the husband dies separate. It has been held by the Privy Council "that where a residue is left undivided upon partition, what is divided goes as separate property; what is undivided follows the family property; that which remains as it was devolves in the old line; that which is changed and becomes separate devolves in the new line. In other words the law of succession follows the nature of the property and of the interest in it" (*a*).

(*a*) Kattama Natchiar *v.* Rajah of Shivagunga, 2 S. W. R. P.C., 31, 39.

CHAPTER VIII.

THE WIDOW'S ESTATE.

Qualifications of her proprietorship—Not a fresh root of descent—Limitation of her disposing power—Subject to qualifications her right is in full proprietorship—Restricted estate of inheritance—Power to aliene her widow's estate—Absolute right of possession and enjoyment—Accumulations of unspent income—Power to aliene the corpus of her husband's estate—Where there is necessity—For religious purposes—With consent of reversioners—Surrender to the next reversioner—Accumulations, and their investment.

WHERE a widow succeeds to the estate of her deceased husband she does so by the law of inheritance and as proprietor, but her proprietorship is subject to qualifications. The most important one is that she does not become a fresh root of descent. Her husband's next heirs as ascertained at her death will take; that is, the succession to her husband opens at her death and not at his, exactly as if he were deemed to live on in the person of his widow. She represents her husband's estate so that decrees duly obtained against her in that capacity will bind his reversionary heirs. But her powers over the estate are subject to many restrictions. A woman takes the estate as now defined, whatever male relation she inherits from. The only exception is as regards a sister and possibly a daughter by the particular form of Hindu law which is applicable in Bombay. The reason of this exception is that the Mayukha is supposed to favour the absolute interest of a female heir. At one time it was supposed that the Mitakshara did so too; but that view has been long abandoned (*a*). The limitations on her disposing

(*a*) See Chotaylall *v.* Chunnolall, L. R. 6 I. A., 15.

power are inseparable from her estate. They do not depend upon the existence of next heirs to the last male proprietor. If they fail, her power of alienation is not enlarged. The Crown as *ultimus hæres* has the same right as any other heir would have to forbid any unauthorised alienation (*a*).

The usual cases of a woman taking what is technically called a widow's estate, are those of a widow or daughter, mother or grandmother, succeeding to any Hindu owner in Bengal, whether joint or separate, or to a separated owner under the Mitakshara. The nature of the estate is the same in all those instances. The law was declared very early in the century under the Bengal school, and as soon as the contention that under the Mitakshara a female heir took an absolute estate was abandoned, her position under that school was assimilated to that in Bengal. In 1819 the Pundits of the Supreme and Sudder Courts of Bengal, not without some opposition from other Pundits, established the doctrine that "the widow, in Bengal, has the entire right of property vested in her both in the movable and immovable estate (*b*); for there is no distinction between them taken in the books in respect of the husband's estate devolving upon her as heir, but that she is legally prohibited from wasting the property so vested in her, and cannot make away with it, except for certain allowable and declared purposes, without the consent of her husband's next male heir; and further considering that even in the use and enjoyment of the property so vested, she is religiously and morally enjoined to use moderation and take the advice of her husband's kindred in her manner of living, but is under no legal disability if she do not take or follow such advice."

(*a*) Collector of Masulipatam *v.* Cavaly Vencata Narainapah, 8 Moore, I. A., 550.

(*b*) Per East, C. J. (1819), in Kasheenath Bysack *v.* Hurrosoondery Dossee, Shamachurn's Vyavastha Darpana, p. 93.

It (*a*) was declared by the Privy Council in the same case, that whatever may be the extent of the widow's power or control over the movable or immovable property of her husband, she is entitled to the possession of both, and cannot be deprived of it by the husband's relations. Her right to the possession is absolute, and cannot be restricted. With regard to the extent of her interest in it and right of dominion over it, the Privy Council laid it down that "she was only entitled to enjoy it according to the rights of a Hindu widow, which rights (that is chiefly the extent of her power of disposition) it was absolutely impossible to define, because it must depend upon the circumstances of that disposition, whenever such disposition should be made, and must be consistent with the law regulating such dispositions."

After that judgment, the Hindu widow's estate was no longer regarded as a mere life-estate, but as a restricted estate of inheritance; and on proof of waste or wrongful alienation by her, the next heirs or the Court would be put in possession as receivers.

A Full Bench decision (*b*) of the High Court at Calcutta decided, after consideration of all the cases, that a conveyance by a Hindu widow "for other than allowable causes" of her husband's estate is not an act of waste which destroys the widow's estate, and vests the property in the reversionary heir; but that the conveyance is binding for the widow's life. This decision was regarded as an innovation at the time; but it is universally accepted. "The reversionary heirs," the Court said, in declaring what is now familiar law, "are not, after the husband's death, bound by the conveyance, but they are not entitled during her lifetime to recover her property either for their own or for the use of the widow, or to compel the

(*a*) See Shamachurn, p. 99, per Lord Gifford.

(*b*) Gobindmonee Dossee *v.* Shamloll Bysack, S. W. R. F. B., 165; and see also Gridharee Singh *v.* Koolahal Singh, 6 S. W. R. P.C., 1, s. c. B. L. R., supp. 48.

restoration of it to her." She has, therefore, an uncontrolled power over the estate so far as her life interest is concerned.

Her absolute right of enjoyment of such life estate follows. She is in no sense a trustee thereof for the benefit of the reversionary heirs. She may spend the income (*a*) and manage (so long as she does not commit waste) the principal as she pleases, and can also give away her savings, so long as they have not passed into what are technically called accumulations; to which latter a special rule is applicable.

With regard to her powers of disposition over the corpus of her husband's either movable or immovable, they only arise under special circumstances—(1) where there is necessity; (2) for religious purposes; (3) with consent of reversioners. With regard to necessity it is impossible to define it, but the most usual instance is that of paying Government revenue or an urgent private debt. The established rule is that the actual existence of present necessity is sufficient to give rise to the power, notwithstanding that it has been brought about by her antecedent mismanagement or extravagance. The rule in Hunoomanpershad's case (*b*) applies to her as well as to the male manager of a family estate; and in the absence of collusion a purchaser or mortgagor is only bound to inquire into the actual existing necessity at the time of the transaction. It is generally admitted that, for religious or charitable purposes, or for those which are supposed to conduce to the spiritual welfare of her husband, she has a larger power of disposition than that which she possesses for purely worldly purposes (*c*). The prohibitions against waste do not include such expenditure as may be deemed beneficial to her husband, as, for example, the performance of his funeral rites, gifts to

(*a*) Hurrydoss Dutt *v.* Sreemutty Uppoornah, 6 Moore, I. A., 433.

(*b*) 6 Moore, I. A., 393.

(*c*) Collector of Masulipatam *v.* Cavaly Vencata Narainapah, 2 W. R., P.C., p. 61.

his relations, the marriage of his daughters, and various charitable acts. "She whose husband is dead," it is said, "should support in proportion to her ability the same persons, and do the same acts in the same manner in which her husband, when living, supported those persons and did those acts. But it is not absolutely necessary that she should fulfil the same voluntary offices which her husband did, such as supporting *Brahmanas* resident in the same town and the like" (*a*).

The third case is where the reversionary heirs consent to the widow's alienation. In that case the difficulty is to ascertain who are the parties whose consent is effectual. Those who are called the reversionary heirs have no vested interest: their rights are contingent upon their surviving the widow, and if they predecease her, the estate at her death may pass to persons who will claim by a title wholly independent of those who have consented. The Privy Council said in one case "the exception in favour of alienation with consent may be due to a presumption of law that where that consent is given, the purpose for which the alienation is made must be proper" (*b*). In another they said "there should be such a concurrence of the members of the family as suffices to raise a presumption that the transaction was a fair one, and one justified by Hindu law" (*c*); and further that the required consent should be of "all those who are likely to be interested in disputing the transaction" (*c*). There is however another principle, for, as a Full Bench of the Bengal High Court held (*d*), it is settled beyond all question by a long current of decisions that a widow may surrender her estate to the next reversioner, so as to bring his estate into possession,

(*a*) Colebrooke's Digest, Book V., Chap. VIII., Section 399, note.

(*b*) Collector of Masulipatam *v.* Cavaly Venkata, 8 Moore, I. A., 551.

(*c*) Raj Lukhee Debia *v.* Gokool Chunder Chowdry, 13 Moore, I. A., 228.

(*d*) Nobokishore *v.* Harinath, I. L. R. 10 Cal., 1102.

and thereby defeat all subsequent interests. Where this principle is accepted it follows that the widow, with the consent of the next reversioner or reversioners, may convey to a third party. The Allahabad High Court dissents from this view. That Court goes so far as to say that if a widow surrenders to the next heir, that does not vest the whole estate in him, but merely the widow's estate (*a*). Perhaps the sound rule may be that, where the immediate reversioners either accept a surrender or consent to the widow's alienation, those who derive their reversionary claim through them are bound, but not those who claim independently (*b*).

These limitations on the widow's disposing power apply to all immovable estate of her husband, whether ancestral or self-acquired. As regards his movable estate, that is subject to the same rule both by the Bengal and the Mitakshara law. In one case the Privy Council considered that there might be a difference in this respect as regards the law administered in the Mithila and in Western and Southern India (*c*). But shortly afterwards it held that "the reasons for the restrictions which the Hindu law imposes on the widow's dominion over her inheritance from her husband, whether founded on her natural dependence on others, her duty to lead an ascetic life, or on the impolicy of allowing the wealth of one family to pass to another, are as applicable to personal property invested so as to yield an income as they are to land. The more ancient texts importing the restriction are general" (*d*).

With regard to a widow's savings out of the income of the estate after it has come to her hands there is some difficulty as to whether they belong to her absolutely, and if so, under what circumstances. The established rule of law is

(*a*) Ramphal Rai *v.* Tula Kuari, I. L. R. 6 All. (F. B.), 116.
(*b*) Muteeoollah *v.* Rohhabinoda, Beng. S. D. A., 1856, p. 604.
(*c*) Musst Thakoor Deyhee *v.* Rai Baluk Ram, 11 Moore, I. A., 139, 175.
(*d*) Bhugwandeen Doobey *v.* Myna Baee, 11 Moore, I. A., 513.

that she may spend or give away her whole income as it arises year by year; also that she may aliene her widow's estate to a stranger. Another rule equally well established is that whatever investments a widow makes out of the income of her husband's estate are an increment to that estate; at least, if they are once carried to the credit of that estate, or mixed up with it, or treated by her as forming part of it. They then become irrevocably accretions thereto, and can only be dealt with by her as if they were part of the original corpus of the estate (*a*). The widow's power over such income as she does not spend is that she may give it either in cash or in the form of an investment made with the plainly apparent intention of at once giving it away. Unless that intention is apparent the investment is *primâ facie* an accretion to the husband's estate. How long she may hold the savings or these investments in suspense is doubtful. Their tendency is to accrete to the corpus of the estate, unless at once disposed of. Possibly the law is not finally ascertained on this subject. If she can aliene the whole widow's estate, thereby giving to the purchaser all accumulations made by him subsequent to his purchase, she is exercising a power which is denied in the case of occasional savings. There are *obiter dicta* in the cases cited below, which favour the widow's disposing power over accumulations, and one of them on p. 66 of L. R. 14 I. A. contemplates her changing the course of succession thereto.

(*a*) See Isri Dutt *v.* Hansbutti, L. R. 10 I. A., 158, and Grose's case, 4 B. L. R., O. C. J., 1, Sheo Lochun Singh *v.* Saheb Singh, L. R. 14 I. A., 63, and Gonda Koer *v.* Kooer Oodey Singh, 14 Beng. L. R., 159, P.C.

CHAPTER IX.

THE LAW OF ALIENATION.—GIFTS.

Gifts—Relinquishment and acceptance—Donee must be in existence—Gift must be followed by possession—Gift may be subject to conditions—Must not create an estate unknown to the Hindu law—*The Tagore case*—Trusts are within the scope of Hindu law—Limitations imposed by Hindu law on the alienation of an absolute title—As to transferee for value taking possession—True owner can make title though dispossessed—Form of alienation—Writing not necessary by the old Hindu law—Prescribed by statute—Construction—Benami transactions.

To complete the law of alienation other than by will it is necessary to consider the law regulating the subject of gifts, and the mode in which a valid alienation is effected.

Relinquishment and acceptance together are necessary in order to effect a valid transfer of property; (*a*) and the condition is added that the relinquishment must be in favour of a sentient being. Acceptance is that act of the donee whereby he recognises the thing given for his own. According to Sir Barnes Peacock's judgment in Tagore *v.* Tagore (*b*), "a gift cannot operate to pass property unless the donee is in existence, so that as soon as the property is relinquished and passes out of the donor it may vest in the donee." Further, "the designation of the donee must be so certain that the latter may be capable of accepting the gift, and that it may be ascertained, immediately the property ceases to be that of the donor, who is the person intended to be benefited and in whom the property given has vested."

(*a*) Dayabhaga, c. I. v. 21, note.

(*b*) 4 Beng. L. R., O. C. J., 188.

The old authorities were clear upon that subject. The idea which runs through that portion of the Dayabhaga which treats of the transfer of property is the two-fold one of constituting the right of one man after annulling the previous right of another. "Heritage," it is said, "signifies 'what is given'; that is, wealth which, on the extinction by death of one man's property in it, becomes the property of another. There is, therefore, nothing to show that, according to Hindu law, after property has ceased by virtue of a gift to be that of the donor, there can be any contingency or uncertainty as to the person in whom it is to vest, or that the property can be so given, whether by will or by alienation *inter vivos*, as to remain in abeyance or *in nubibus* until the donee come into existence. And with regard to immovable property, there is a text of Yajnavalkya which especially enjoins publicity of acceptance; that is, acceptance in the presence of witnesses. Jagannatha adds that a written contract of gift is proper, and that in the want of that the donation should be attested. He also says that, 'in the case of gift, acceptance alone generates property. Accordingly, an inanimate being can have no property, through the want of the requisite acts, from the effort with which an acquisition originates until final acceptance.'"

From the rule as to acceptance arose the further rule that a valid gift must be followed by the possession of the donee. Such change of possession is effected by receipt of rent by the donee, by delivery to him of the deed of gift or other documents of title, or in case of his incapacity by the donor undertaking to hold possession in trust for him. A gift to the donee of the right to take possession, though not immediately acted upon, is sufficient (*a*). Where at the time the gift takes effect the donee is in the womb or is not yet

(*a*) Kali Das Mullick *v.* Kanhya Lal Pundit, L. R. 11 I. A., 218.

adopted, an exception is made, the fictitious existence being assumed to be real.

If the gift is effectual, it may be subject to conditions; so long as they are not immoral, illegal, or repugnant to the nature of the gift. Such conditions would be void unless they formed the consideration for the gift, in which case the gift itself would fail.

A gift will be invalid which creates any estate which is unknown to or forbidden by Hindu law.

The leading case on the exercise of the power of alienation according to Hindu law is the well-known Tagore case (*a*) decided by the Privy Council in 1872. It lays down these general principles as affecting the transfer of property wherever law exists, which cannot therefore be lost sight of in regulating transfers by Hindus. (1) A private individual who attempts by gift or will to make property inheritable otherwise than as the law directs is assuming to legislate, and the gift must fail, and the inheritance take place as the law directs; (2) with reference to transfers by gift a benignant construction is to be used, the real meaning shall be enforced to the extent and in the form which the law allows; (3) all estates of inheritance created by gift or will, so far as they are inconsistent with the general law of inheritance, are void as such.

It follows from these principles of universal application that a Hindu cannot so dispose of his property as to make it inheritable in the mode directed by English law. Accordingly by Hindu law no Hindu can succeed under gift or will to estates described in terms which in English law would designate estates tail. He can succeed thereunder to a gift for life or to an absolute gift, for both classes of gift are recognised by Hindu law; provided he is either in fact or in contemplation of law in existence at the time when the gift takes effect, that is in the

(*a*) L. R., I. A. Supp., 47.

case of a will at the death of the testator. In the term existing in contemplation of law are included children in embryo and children subsequently adopted.

It is convenient here to observe that it was decided in that case, after some controversy on the subject, that trusts of various kinds including implied trusts are within the scope of Hindu law, since they have been recognised and acted on in many cases. But it was also held that a Hindu cannot under the guise of an unnecessary trust of inheritance indirectly create beneficiary estates of a character unauthorised by Hindu law. If they cannot be created directly, neither can they be indirectly created with the intervention of a trust. Wherever a trust is created with that object it will only be sustained to the extent and for the purpose of giving effect to those beneficiary interests which the law recognises. The alienation is valid to that extent. If it has been made by will, then as regards the residue undisposed of in a way which the law allows, there is intestacy. If it has been made by deed *inter vivos*, then so far as it fails to take effect there is a resulting trust in favour of the grantor. The Tagore case was one in which a Hindu testator, apparently intending to disinherit his eldest son, left the residue of his estate to A for life. So far it took effect. But when this life estate determined, the gift over was in favour of persons unborn at the death of the testator. So far it did not take effect. Further, there were successive limitations describing inheritances in tail male as understood in English law. These were held to be void and of no effect. The will, therefore, only operated to create a life estate in the residue. As regards the estate which remained after the determination of the life interest, the testator had failed to declare any intention which was legally capable of being carried into effect, and in consequence the heir at law was entitled as under an intestacy.

The following passages from the judgment of the Privy Council in the Tagore case are of great importance as describing the limitations upon the power of alienation, where that power is so unfettered as it is in Bengal. An absolute power of gift or devise means that a man can denude himself of all proprietary right, but his power to control the exercise and devolution of that proprietary right after he has parted with it is strictly limited. He cannot annex to it conditions inconsistent with its enjoyment, nor can he prescribe a mode of devolution contrary to law, nor can he carve out different interests in it except as between donees, all of whom are in legal existence at the time the alienation takes effect. The judgment lays down these rules :—

"If a gift confers an estate upon a man with words imperfectly describing the kind of inheritance, but showing that it was intended that he should have an estate of inheritance, the language would be read as conferring an estate inheritable as the law directs." In other words, it would be assumed that he was dealing with his estate in accordance with his legal powers, and the intention to exceed those powers and act illegally would have to be clearly manifested in order to render the gift invalid either entirely or so far as it was illegal. The judgment proceeds :—

"If an estate were given to a man simply without express words of inheritance, it would, in the absence of a conflicting context, carry by Hindu law (as under the present state of the law it does by will in England) an estate of inheritance. If there were added to such a gift an imperfect description of it as a gift of inheritance, not excluding the inheritance imposed by the law, an estate of inheritance would pass.

"If, again, the gift were in terms of an estate inheritable according to law, with superadded words restricting the power of transfer which the law annexes to that estate, the restriction would be rejected as being repugnant, or rather as being an attempt to take away the power of transfer which the law attaches to the estate which the giver has sufficiently shown his intention to create, though he adds a qualification which the law does not recognise.

"If, on the other hand, the gift were to a man and his heirs to be selected from a line other than that specified by law, expressly excluding the legal course of inheritance; as, for instance, if an estate were granted to a man and his eldest nephew, and the eldest nephew of such eldest nephew, and so forth, for ever to take as his heirs, to the exclusion of all other heirs, and without any of the persons so taking having the power to dispose of the estate during his lifetime; here, inasmuch as an inheritance so described is not legal, such a gift cannot take effect except in favour of such persons as could take under a gift to the extent to which the gift is consistent with the law. The first taker would in this case take for his lifetime, because the giver had at least that intention. He could not take more because the language is inconsistent with his having any different inheritance from that which the gift attempts to confer, and that estate of inheritance which it confers is void.

"It follows that all estates of inheritance created by gift or will, so far as they are inconsistent with the general law of inheritance, are void as such, and that by Hindu law no person can succeed thereunder as heir to the estates described in the terms, which in English law would designate estates tail."

With regard to the distinctions between transfers for value and gifts, as regards the necessity for possession being taken by the transferee for value, there are two classes of cases (1) where the vendor is out of possession and cannot give it though he has a right to it, (2) where he is in possession and does not give it. As to (1), the High Court of Bengal has upheld such transfer, and allowed the transferee to sue in ejectment (*a*); the High Court at Bombay has decided to the contrary (*b*). As to (2), it has been decided in Madras that a sale without delivery of possession is valid, as against a subsequent sale by the same owner followed by possession (*c*), regardless apparently of the subsequent sale being without notice of the prior one. The decisive case now upon this subject is that of Kalidas Mullick *v.* Kanhya Lal (*d*), where the Privy Council say that there is "no reason why a gift or contract of sale of property, whether movable or immovable, if it is not of a nature which makes the giving effect to it contrary to public policy, should not operate to give to the donee or purchaser a right to obtain possession." In other words, the true owner is not prevented from making title merely because he is wrongfully kept out of possession.

As to the form of alienation, writing was never necessary under the old Hindu law to the validity of any transfer of either movable or immovable property. Nor were any technical words necessary. But on this subject the provisions of the various Registration Acts and of the Transfer of Property Act (IV. of 1882) must now be attended to; and writing in many cases has become necessary under statute law and to enable registration.

As respects writings, whether deeds of conveyance or contracts, the rule of law is that they ought to be most liberally construed. "The form of expression, the literal sense, is not so much to be regarded as the real meaning of the parties which the transaction discloses" (*e*).

(*a*) Gungahurry *v.* Raghubram, 14 B. L. R., 307. Nittyanund *v.* Shamachurn, 23 S. W. R., 163. Auloch *v.* Auloch, 25 S. W. R., 48.

(*b*) Lalubhai *v.* Bai Amrit, I. L. R. 2 Bomb., 299. Kachu *v.* Kachoba, 10 Bomb., H. C. R., 491.

(*c*) Ramasami *v.* Marimuttu, I. L. R. 6 Mad., 404.

(*d*) L. R. 11 I. A., 218.

(*e*) Hunooman Persad Pandey *v.* Mussamut Babooee Munraj Koonwaree, 6 Moore, I. A., 411.

For instance, no words of inheritance are necessary in a deed of conveyance in order to continue to a Hindu's heirs the interest which he takes under it in the estate conveyed (*a*).

Contrary, however, to the ordinary rule of law that a man's signature by way of attestation to the due execution of a deed does not fix him with a knowledge of its contents, it has been held, and is now established law, that the attestation by a reversioner of the execution by a Hindu widow of a deed alienating any portion of her husband's property, not merely fixes him with a knowledge of its contents, but shows an acquiescence on his part in her alienation, and he will not be afterwards allowed to impeach it on the ground of waste (*b*). The rule would seem to rest upon the principle that the fact of a conveyance of any sort being made by such a person is quite sufficient to put a reversioner on inquiry and on his guard, and that if he not merely abstains from inquiry but lends his name to the transaction, it would be opening the door to serious frauds to allow him afterwards to plead his ignorance of its true nature and effect. The consent, moreover, need not be given in writing (*c*).

It is the established practice of the Courts in India in cases of contract to require satisfactory proof that consideration has been actually received according to the terms of the contract. It has never been held that a contract made under seal of itself imports that there has been a sufficient consideration for the agreement (*d*).

With regard to benami transactions, that is where property of one man is placed in the name of another, they are part of the custom of the country recognised as valid by the Indian Courts and by the Privy Council. In all cases even when a

(*a*) Anundmoye Dossee *v.* John Doe *d.* E. I. Company, 4 S. W. R. P.C., 51; and 8 Moore, I. A., 43.

(*b*) Gopaul C. Manna *v.* Gourmonee Dossee, 6 S. W. R., 52.

(*c*) Mohesh C. Bose *v.* Ugra Kant, 24 S. W. R., 127.

(*d*) Rajah Sahib Prahlad Sen *v.* Baboo Budhu Singh, 2 B. L. R. P.C., 111.

parent takes or places his property in the name of his child, the rule is that there is a resulting trust in favour of the true owner. In all cases, therefore, the true criterion is with whose funds was the property purchased. The man who found and paid the purchase money is *primâ facie* the owner. But the evidence as to the origin of the purchase money must be clear in all disputed cases; when once established, the fictitious owner or benamidar cannot rely upon apparent acts of ownership by him as evidence of an adverse possession, for the said acts followed the apparent ownership which was consented to by both parties.

When once a transaction is shown to be genuine, the Courts will give effect to the real title as against the fictitious one in suits between them. Third persons, such as creditors, can insist upon ascertaining the true state of the title, and having effect given to their claims on that footing.

The exception is where the effect of placing the property in the name of a fictitious owner has effected a fraud upon innocent persons. If it has, as for instance where the benamidar has sold or mortgaged the property standing in his name to a purchaser or mortgagee who had no notice, either direct or constructive of the true state of the title, the true owner cannot recover (*a*).

The more frequent case is when property of a debtor has been placed in the hands of a benamidar to shield it from creditors. Then after the creditors are defrauded, the true owner sues the benamidar to get it back. In the earlier cases the Courts refused relief, but finally the rule provided that by doing so they themselves assisted in a different fraud by practically giving the estate to one who was not entitled to it and was not intended to have it (*b*).

(*a*) Ramcoomar Koondoo *v.* McQucen, L. R. I. A. Supp., 44.

(*b*) Sreemutty Debia *v.* Bimola, 21 S. W. R., 422.

CHAPTER X.

The Members of the Joint Family—Their Civil Status.

Civil status—Caste—Ceremonies of regeneration—Tonsure—Upanayana—Marriage - Rights of wife—Re-marriage of widows—Act XV. of 1856—Status of illegitimate son—Majority—Act IX. of 1875—Guardianship.

We now pass from the joint family and the considerations to which it gives rise, both under the Dayabhaga and Mitakshara systems to the subject of the personal rights and duties which devolve upon individuals. The rules which determine the civil *status* of each, that is his position in the eye of Hindu law, *e.g.*, his age of majority, his legitimacy, his marriage, his capacity to be adopted and so forth, are derived from the doctrines of religion, and it is not always easy to distinguish the precepts which have the sanction only of religion from the rules which have the force of law.

At his birth there is ascribed to him by law the state or position involved in the possession of a particular caste.

The *caste* to which he belongs influences his legal position, for each *caste* has its special rules, still to some extent and for some purposes recognised by law, which affect only its own members. Religious teaching separates the regenerate or twice-born Hindu from the unregenerate Hindu, who is still affected by the taint of sin which he contracted in the womb. The only regenerating ceremony for a Sudra, or a woman of whatever caste, is marriage. In the other three castes, marriage is the final ceremony which completes the regeneration of a male Hindu. It unalterably fixes him as a member of the family in which he was born, after which, under no circumstances whatever, can he be affiliated in any other family, or to any other father, away from and destroying his affiliation to his natural father.

It originally marked the period at which a Hindu attained his majority.

There are eight successive ceremonies which are necessary in order that a Hindu boy of the three superior castes, *viz.*, the *Brahmana*, the *Kshatriya*, and *Vaisya* castes, may attain regeneration. Though Hindu law, especially as recognised and administered in English Courts, does not in general regard their performance or omission as affecting the legal position of a Hindu, yet they are all of more or less importance. Besides completing the work of regeneration, they successively strengthen the tie which binds the boy to the family in which they are performed; and two of them, the ceremony of tonsure and the ceremony of investiture with the Brahminical thread, called upanayana, have often been discussed in Courts of law, especially with reference to their effect on a boy's capacity for adoption, *i.e.*, the legal ability to be transferred to and affiliated in a family other than that of birth.

The two last-mentioned ceremonies are alone of legal interest. The rite of tonsure is of importance in securing the affiliation of a child in the family of his birth, or to his natural father. In case of adoption, it is important that it should be performed in the family of the adopter, in order to secure his sonship to the adopted father. The family name is used in the rite, and its use is essential to its efficacy. "The coronal locks," it is said, "of the boy must be made with the enunciation of his patriarchal tribe." And according to Nanda Pandita, "that son, who is initiated under the family name of his natural father, unto the ceremony of tonsure, does not become the son of another man."

Upanayana consists of the investiture of the child with the marks of his class. Its performance is an absolute bar to his adoption into another family (*a*). Marriage is the final ceremony. There were eight forms of it, all of which are obsolete, except the Brahma and Asura forms, the latter in use chiefly amongst Sudras. The form of marriage sometimes affects the devolution of Stridhan. It is an indissoluble contract, as well as a religious sacrament. The contract itself is considered to be complete and irrevocable after the bride and bridegroom have joined hands, after having walked seven steps hand in hand, during the recital of certain prayers (*b*). Only one wife is enjoined, but there is nothing in Hindu law or usage to render polygamy illegal (*c*).

The restrictions upon the right to contract marriage depend upon considerations of relationship or caste. As regards the latter, the old rule was that a woman may not marry a man of a caste beneath her; a man may marry in his own caste or an inferior one (*d*). According to Mr. Sutherland in his synopsis, marriage with one unequal in class is prohibited at the present day (*e*). But the High Court in Madras (*f*) in a case affirmed by the Privy Council (*g*) stated the existing rule as follows:—" The general law applicable to all the classes or tribes does not seem opposed to marriage between individuals of different sects or divisions of the same class or tribe; and even as regards marriage between individuals of a different class or tribe, the law appears to be no more than directory. Although it recommends and inculcates a marriage with a woman of equal class as a preferable description, yet the marriage

(*a*) Dattaka Mimansa IV., 30, 56, and Dattaka Chandrika, s. 2, v. 31.
(*b*) Jagannatha's Digest, Bk. IV., c. 4, s. 3, v. 175.
(*c*) Virasvami Chetti *v.* Appasvami Chetti, 1 Madras, H. C. 375.
(*d*) Menu, ix., 149, 157.
(*e*) Synopsis, Heading ii.
(*f*) Pandaiya Telaver *v.* Puli Telaver, 1 Madr., H. C. 478.
(*g*) 13 Moore, I. A. 141.

of a man with a woman of a lower caste or tribe than himself appears not to be an invalid marriage rendering the issue illegitimate." A wife when mature is bound to live in her husband's house (*a*), and he is bound to maintain her; if she quits for other than allowable cause she has no claim to a separate maintenance (*b*).

The wife's power to pledge her husband's credit, or to render him liable on her contracts, on the ground of an implied agency, is the same in Hindu as in English law. "A person dealing with a Hindu wife and seeking to charge her husband must show either that the wife is living with her husband and managing the household affairs, in which case an implied agency to buy necessaries is presumed, or he must show the existence of such a state of things as would warrant her in living apart from her husband and claiming support and maintenance, when of course the law would give her an implied authority to bind him for necessaries supplied to her during such separation, in the event of his not providing her with maintenance" (*c*). It has been held by the Madras High Court that the supercession of a wife by a second marriage does not justify her separation from her husband, and cannot of itself give her implied authority as his agent to bind him for debts incurred for necessaries (*d*).

With regard to the re-marriage of widows, whatever difference of opinion there may have been amongst the older authorities (Menu being strongly opposed to it), local custom occasionally sanctioned it. Wherever it was illegal it effected a forfeiture of the widow's estate; and in some instances, as in Bombay, even a legal second marriage had the same effect.

(*a*) Dadaji *v.* Rukmabai, I. L. R., 10 Bomb. 301, reversing I. L. R. 9 Bomb. 529.

(*b*) Kullyanessuree *v.* Dwarkanath, 6 S. W. R., 116.

(*c*) 1 Madr. H. C., 377.

(*d*) Ibid., 378.

Act XV. of 1856 was passed to enable the re-marriage of widows, which is accordingly now legal in all cases; with this important proviso that all her rights in her husband's estate, whether by way of maintenance or by inheritance to her husband or his lineal successors, or by virtue of any will or testamentary provision conferring upon her, without express permission to re-marry, only a limited interest in such property without power of alienation shall upon her re-marriage cease and determine as if she had died. The next heirs of her husband, or other persons entitled to the property on her death, will at once succeed to the same. The forfeiture, however, is limited to existing rights; if after her re-marriage succession to the son of her first husband opens to her, she will take (*a*). A widow who has ceased to be a Hindu at the time of her re-marriage will forfeit her husband's estate (*b*).

With regard to the status of an illegitimate son in a Hindu family, all the analogies (*c*) of Hindu law are against the view of a bastard taken by the law of England, which law in that respect is founded upon the doctrine of Christianity. The right of inheritance to their father's estate, which formerly belonged (*d*) to illegitimate sons in the Sudra caste, is still retained by them (*e*). But in the three superior castes, an illegitimate son has long ceased to possess a right to inherit. Nevertheless, he is not, as in English law, *quasi nullius filius*, but his *status* as a son in the family, and his right to maintenance, are secured to him. Further than that, illegitimacy is no taint or disqualification for *caste* in the individual and his children (*f*). But it depends upon the *caste* of the father, whether it disables a man from

(*a*) Akora Suth *v.* Boreani, 2 Beng. L. R. A. C. J., 199.

(*b*) Matangini Gupta *v.* Ram Rutton Roy, I. L. R. 19 Cal., 289.

(*c*) Mayna Bai *v.* Uttaram, 2 Madras H. C., p. 196, 203.

(*d*) Mitakshara, Chapter I., Section 12; 1 Strange's Hindu Law, p. 132.

(*e*) 3 Beng. L. R. P. C., 4; s. c., 13 Moore, I. A. 141.

(*f*) Pandaiya Telaver *v.* Puli Telaver, 1 Madras H. C., p. 478.

inheriting. If that father's caste is above the Sudra, the illegitimate son cannot inherit, even though the caste is one of the mixed classes between the second and third of Menu's divisions.

The completion of the regenerating ceremonies marks, according to Hindu law, the period at which the boy ceases to be under tutelage, and is considered to have attained the age of discretion. The completion of the sixteenth year generally throughout India is the age at which, according to the original shasters, a Hindu attained majority. In Bengal, the commencement of the sixteenth year, *i.e.*, the completion of the fifteenth, was the age at which the disabilities of minority cease. Various authorities, including Raghunandana, the great authority of Bengal, concur in fixing the end of the fifteenth year as the limit of minority. And Jagannatha, in his Digest, expressly mentions the end of the fifteenth year; for the annotation of Srikrishna to the Dayabhaga seems to have fixed the rule as applicable in Bengal.

The rule was soon infringed by the legislature. Minors were declared disqualified for the management of their estates, and in 1793 the age of majority was postponed from the end of the 15th to the end of the 18th year as regards proprietors of estates paying revenue to Government (*a*). Again, all persons to whom Act XL. of 1858 were deemed minors till eighteen. The uncertainty thus introduced as to the age of majority led to the passing of Act IX. of 1875, which lays down the rule for all persons domiciled in British India that eighteen is the age of majority, except when the minor is actually under the Court of Wards, or has ever had a guardian appointed for him by a Court of Justice, in which event his minority lasts till the age of twenty-one. The Act does not affect any person in respect of marriage, dower, divorce, or adoption.

(*a*) Reg. X. of 1793, s. 28.

During minority, the disabilities may be considered to be the same amongst Hindus as amongst those subject to English law. They are so held to be in practice. Very little is to be found in purely Hindu law books on the subject of guardianship. The subject is regulated by statutes of which the chief are the various Court of Wards Acts passed for the different presidencies and Act XL. of 1858.

CHAPTER XI.

THE LAW OF WILLS.

Early history of wills—Not of foreign importation—First established under English rule in Bengal—In Madras—In Bombay—Extent of testamentary power—Act XXI. of 1870—What property may be devised—Who may take under a will—Testamentary power is the creation of Hindu law—Its limitations are those prescribed by Hindu law—Illegal conditions annexed to a devise—Perpetuities—Probate.

WILLS are said to have been unknown to early Hindu law, which has no word to express the idea of testamentary distribution. The selection of a successor by a dying *kurta* of a Hindu family contrary to the rule by which the eldest surviving member of the family would become its head, and the exercise of the power or faculty of adoption were expedients frequently practised, and show that Hindus were familiar in very early times with a distortion of the ordinary family descent. The *onoomutteeputtro,* or writing whereby a husband empowers his widow after his death to adopt for him, is a document of testamentary character and incidents, aud is often treated as a will in the reported cases. Mohunts of temples also frequently appointed, and continue to do so, their successors either by word of mouth or in writing; the appointments taking effect from the moment of their death.

A Hindu, therefore, in very early times must have been to some extent familiar with the control by a living person of the posthumous disposition of his property. The practice of making such dispositions must have grown in course of time, for it seems to be firmly established that Hindu wills are not of foreign importation. They appear to have been in use not merely in Bengal, but throughout India before the establishment of English Courts. Mr. Montriou has pointed out in his "Essay upon the Hindu Will," on the authority of a statement of the Procureur-General, that at Pondicherry wills of Hindus were recognised in the French settlement from the commencement of the French rule. From the time of the establishment of the Mayors' Courts in Calcutta and Madras, probates of wills were granted by those Courts. The Supreme Court of Calcutta granted probate of a will of a Hindu within a few months after the Court met for the transaction of business, that is, as early as January, 1776. Mr. Montriou has reported a case in which Sir William Jones upheld a will as valid, apparently with the concurrence of the pundits, and certainly without any opposition from them (*a*). Again, the will of the Nuddea Raja was submitted to the pundits of various localities towards the end of last century, viz., to those of Nuddea, Benares, Gya, Dinajepore, Moorshedabad, and Dacca. Amongst them was Jagannatha Tarkapauchanana, the author of the Digest. Not one of these pundits denied the right of a Hindu to dispose of his property by will. They differed as to its effect, but they took for granted the existence of a power of testamentary disposition (*b*).

Sir Thomas Strange, in the second volume (*c*) of his Hindu Law, has given opinions of the pundits of Bellari, Madras, Masulipatam, Chittore, Chingleput, and Vizagapatam, each upon a different case. They all of them assent expressly or impliedly to the doctrine that a Hindu has power to make a will. And Mr. Justice Norman (*d*) pointed out that wills are also found in the records of the Zillah Courts at Bombay, as appears from numerous cases in Boradaile's Reports.

(*a*) Monee Lall Baboo *v.* Gopee Dutt, Montriou's Cases, Hindu Law, p. 295.

(*b*) Montriou's Cases, Hindu Law, Appendix, Note XVI.

(*c*) Pp. 417—427.

(*d*) 4 B. L. R., O. C., p. 217.

As a matter of antiquarian interest the balance of testimony is in favour of the antiquity of Hindu wills. But the English Courts seem for a long time to have been perplexed with them. They first became established in Bengal, where the power of alienation was more extensive. Regulation IV. of 1793 recognised them; and Regulation XXXVI. of that year provided for their registry. In Madras they seem to have been treated as on the same footing with gifts *inter vivos.* The local Regulation (V. of 1829) recited that wills were unknown and enacted that they should have no legal force, except so far as they were in accordance with Hindu law as accepted in Madras. In Bombay the same reluctance to recognise wills was displayed by the Courts, but the practice of making them was too general to be disregarded. But in 1866 (*a*) Westropp (C. J.) said that they had always been recognised by the Supreme Court, and returns showed that they were made in all parts of the Mofussil, and had on several occasions been acted upon by the Appellate Court.

The extent of testamentary power amongst Hindus, whatever difficulty there may have been about it in former times, is now settled by judicial decision and express legislation. That power relates first to the subject over which it is exercised; second, to the persons in whose favour it may be exercised, and the nature of the estate which they may take. Throughout Bengal a Hindu who is the absolute owner of property may dispose of it by will as he pleases, whether it is ancestral or not (*b*), as resolved by all the judicial authorities in Calcutta, as well of the Supreme as of the Sudder Court.

Act XXI. of 1870 (Hindu Wills Act) is to the same effect. It extends to Hindus the sections of the Indian Succession Act, 1865, which relate to wills; with these limitations, that

(*a*) Narottam *v.* Narsandas, 3 Bomb. H. C., A. C. J. 8.

(*b*) Dictum of the Privy Council in 6 Moore, I. A., 344; and the Tagore case, L. R., Ind. App., supp. 31.

he cannot devise what he could not have alienated *inter vivos*, and cannot deprive any person of his legal right to maintenance, and "nothing herein contained shall affect any law of adoption or intestate succession."

Under the Mitakshara law, all that a Hindu can dispose of by will is his separate and self-acquired estate. If by the death of all his coparceners he holds in severalty what was joint estate, he may devise it so as to defeat remote heirs (*a*). A woman cannot bequeath any part of her widow's estate, but she can dispose of her stridhana by will. A coparcener even in Madras and Bombay, where he may dispose of his undivided share by sale, may not do so by will, for the coparcener's right by survivorship will be paramount to that of the devisee.

The principle which regulates the extent of the testamentary power, both as regards the subject of the devisee and the character of the disposition, is that laid down by the Privy Council in Sonatun Bysack *v.* Sreemutty Juggutsoondery Dossee (*b*), "that the extent of the testamentary power of disposition by Hindus must be regulated by the Hindu law." In other words, the Privy Council treated it as a branch of Hindu law, to be regulated by principles to be found in that law, and not by the application of rules deducible from any other system or founded on general policy.

That was not the doctrine which had found favour in India. Even in the case in which the Privy Council so ruled, the Supreme Court had treated the testamentary power of Hindus as engrafted on their law by custom, as existing subject to those restraints *which the general policy of the law* imposes. The same expression was used in a later case (*c*).

In another case the Supreme Court considered that a Hindu testamentary disposition (altering rules of succession in per-

(*a*) Beer Pertab *v.* Maharajah Rajender, 12 Moore, I. A., 38.

(*b*) 8 Moore, I. A., 85.

(*c*) Sreemutty Juggutsoondery Dossee *v.* Manickchund Bysack, 1 Boulnois, 271.

petuity) of land partly situated in Chinsurah, which at the time was a Dutch settlement, and partly in British possessions, was bad in the one case because English law forbade the creation of a perpetuity, and good in the other because Roman Dutch law allowed it (*a*). The Privy Council, however, in another case repeated that Hindu wills were firmly established, "but it would be to apply a very false and mischievous principle if it were held that the nature and extent of that power can be governed by any analogy to the law of England" (*b*).

It is a fallacy to treat the devising power of a Hindu as absolute, and then to inquire what are the restraints upon it imposed by general policy or by analogy to other laws. The power itself is the creature of Hindu law, and its limitations are those which Hindu law prescribes in all cases of alienation.

The general principle therefore applicable under the Mitakshara is that a devise cannot prevail against rights by survivorship. Those who would take by inheritance can be ousted by a valid testamentary disposition; coparceners who take by survivorship take by a title paramount to the testator.

Secondly, as to the persons in whose favour a will may be made, and what estate they may take, the Tagore case before referred to (*c*) is the leading authority on this subject. A devisee must be in existence, either actually or in contemplation of law, at the death of the testator. He cannot take any estate unauthorised by Hindu law either directly or indirectly through the intervention of a trust. Trusts are recognised by Hindu law, or a devisee may take subject to the beneficial ownership being vested in another, so far as such beneficial ownership is one which Hindu law recognises. If any limitation violates Hindu law, either as regards the person who is to

(*a*) Luckunchunder Seal *v.* Horomony Dossee, 1 Boulnois, 211.

(*b*) Bhoobunmoye Debia *v.* Ramkishore Acharjee, 3 S. W. R. P.C., 15.

(*c*) See Chap. X.

take or the quantum of estate or interest which is taken, it will be void, and not merely void in itself, but it will render void all subsequent limitations. Persons may take successive life estates provided they are in existence at the death of the testator. For a testator is allowed by Hindu law to give his property, either by way of remainder or by way of executory bequest, upon an event which is to happen, if at all, immediately on the close of a life in being (*a*).

A Hindu cannot give by will any greater estate than the law allows him to do *inter vivos*. He cannot create an estate unknown to the Hindu law, nor can he assume to legislate in any other way, or, for instance, by prescribing a course of succession unknown to that law. He cannot direct that his estate should go in an order of succession different from the legal one. He cannot prescribe a new order of succession, as, for instance, one which should exclude females or adopted sons (*b*). That would be to legislate. A testator can only dispose of his property by a valid exercise of testamentary power. Where he does so to that extent he overrides the law of inheritance, but if he fails to do so the law of intestate inheritance will dispose of the estate; and any negative directions that it shall not devolve in the way which the law directs, or that it shall devolve by some rule contrary to that law, will be disregarded. So also trusts to accumulate the proceeds of property have been held invalid; the condition is an illegal one (*c*). Conditions against alienation or partition cannot be imposed. Nor can the enjoyment of an estate once given be postponed in a manner contrary to law, as, for instance, beyond the period of minority, or in such way that the estate remains without a beneficial owner.

(*a*) Soorjeemoney Dossee *v.* Denobundoo Mullick, 9 Moore, I. A. 135.

(*b*) Kumar Tarakeswar *v.* Kumar Shoshi, L. R. 10 I. A. 51. Surya Rao *v.* Gungadhara, L. R. 13, I. A. 97.

(*c*) Kumara Asima *v.* Kumara Krishna 2 B. L. B. (O. C. J.), 11.

As regards the invalidity of perpetuities, the difficulty which formerly prevailed on that subject was that the Courts in India laid it down that the English rule against perpetuities was not engrafted as Hindu law. As soon as the doctrine of the Privy Council prevailed that "the extent of the testamentary power of disposition by Hindus must be regulated by Hindu law," it was obvious that Hindu law did not authorise perpetuities, and consequently that a Hindu testator could not create them.

With regard to probate of wills, no right as executor or legatee can be established in any Court of Justice under a Hindu will unless probate or letters of administration shall have been granted (*a*). By virtue of the Probate Act (V. of 1881), which at present contains the law on the subject of probates and administrations, the executor or administrator as such is the legal personal representative of the testator and statutory owner of the property to which he was entitled at his death.

(*a*) Hindu Wills Act, 1870, incorporating sect. 187 of Act X. of 1865.

CHAPTER XII.

Religious Endowments.

Religious ceremonies—Right and capacity to perform them—Not enforceable at law—Guru—Purohit—No legal obligation to contribute to expenses of joint worship — Dewutter property—Who can endow — Law of endowments—Sebaits—Pallas—Devolution of the trust — Regulation XIX. of 1810—Act XX. of 1863.

The Hindu joint family is joint in food, worship, and estate; and the subjects of religious ceremonies and worship are a part of Hindu law. For the personal *status* and proprietary right of a Hindu, and even the school of law to which he is amenable, turn upon, or at least are connected with, the observance of religious ceremonies. Some of these ceremonies, therefore, cannot be disregarded in dealing with Hindu law; and with regard to the family, one of the first subjects to be attended to is its relative position to the ministers of religion.

Although Courts of Law do not, as a general rule, discuss the disabilities which arise from the non-performance by a Hindu of religious ceremonies, leaving those ceremonies to the cognizance of the authorities or spiritual guide of his family or *caste*, yet in respect of some of them they affect, or have been long held to affect, the legal *status*,—as for example, the capacity to be adopted. The law of adoption has never been free from the influence and effect of the religious observances which mark the progress of a Hindu in the three upper castes to a state of regeneration. The law of succession to the estate of a deceased is based in all the schools, and, according to the school of Bengal, exclusively upon the religious system, which provides for the performance of various rites and ceremonies in honour not merely of the deceased, but of his ancestors; one of the main objects in view, in regulating the order of succession, being to provide for the due celebration of those religious observances.

Although the non-performance, or the incapacity to perform some of the religious observances enjoined by the shasters, may impose disabilities on the individual who thus fails in his religious obligations, yet it does not appear that there is any recognised legal duty to perform them such as the Courts would interfere to enforce directly or indirectly. "The duty," said Sir Colley Scotland (*a*), "of individuals to submit to and perform certain religious observances in accordance with the ritual or conventional practice of their race or sect, is, in the absence of express legal recognition and provision, of imperfect obligation of a moral, not a civil, nature. Of such obligations the present Civil Courts cannot take cognizance. And it is of great importance, I think, in this country, that the Courts exercising their civil jurisdiction, as now provided, should carefully guard against entertaining suits in respect of mere ritual observances and the conduct of the various kinds of native religious worship and ceremonies, and of what, as incident thereto, may be due to the sacred character or the religious rank and position of individuals. With such matters the Courts cannot properly deal, and if their jurisdiction extended to interference in them, the law would, I fear, be made instrumental in upholding and continuing the ceremonials and superstitious observances of idol-worship, for the benefit merely of the few who profit by them." Although the Courts cannot, or do not, enforce the performance of rites,—say for example of tonsure, or the *upanayana*, they sometimes, to a limited extent, take cognizance of them as affecting the *status* of the

(*a*) Striman Sadogopa *v.* Kristna Tatachariyar, 1 Madras High Court Reports, p. 301.

individual. They do not compel a man to perform the *shraddha* of his ancestors, but they have regard to his right or duty to do so, as it affects the devolution of property, or creates a necessity for the disbursement of ancestral funds.

The guru is the spiritual guide of a family, and has authority which extends to expel a man from his caste. The Purohits conduct worship and all ceremonies. With regard to their legal relations to their jujmans or parishioners, which at one time extended to make the office of Purohit hereditary, the doctrine was established in 1850 (*a*) that *Purohits'* fees were partly voluntary, and partly payment for work and labour done; but were no longer the subject of partition on the ground of hereditary right, although they might be the subject of a partnership account. And in a later year (*b*), the Sudder Court of Bengal ruled that, although, under the Hindu law, there was no doubt that the office of a *Purohit* was, to a certain extent, an hereditary office, yet the Courts would refuse to interfere except when their services were the subject of contract.

Hindus, moreover, are not compellable in law to perform the moral obligation which custom and usage impose of supporting the worship of the family idols, even though they are in possession of the family estate. Co-sharers in ancestral estate cannot be compelled to contribute to expenses so incurred against their will (*c*).

The ordinary method of providing for the support of idols, priests, and worship is by endowment, by the dedication of certain property to an idol, or to a temple, or to the maintenance of Brahmins, or to other religious purposes, which property is thenceforth known by the name of *dewutter* property. Such endowments are recognised, so long as they appear to have

(*a*) Hurgobind Surma *v.* Bhowaneepershad Shah (13th June, 1850), S. D. Decisions, Vol. VI., p. 296; and Ramakant Surma and others *v.* Gobindchunder Surma (13th May, 1852), S. D. Decisions, Vol. VIII., p. 398.

(*b*) Jowahur Misser *v.* Bhagoo Misser, 13 S. D. Decisions, p. 362.

(*c*) Shamloll Sett *v.* Hurrosoonderee Gooptu, 5 S. W. R., p. 29.

been *bonâ fide* made, and are, undoubtedly, encouraged by Hindu law. They must, however, be real and not nominal endowments (*a*); the criterion being the publicity of the dedication or graut, and the appropriation of the rents, issues, and profits to the purposes for which the grant purported to have been made. As a general rule (*b*), written evidence of an endowment will be required. Its absence, however, is not necessarily fatal, provided all the circumstances of the case place the fact of endowment beyond a doubt. Amongst those circumstances the fact that the proceeds of the property have been applied to the support of an idol is strong, but not always conclusive, evidence that the idol has been endowed with such property.

In the case of lands so dedicated before the grant of the dewanny in 1765, they cannot be subjected to the payment of Government revenue (*c*).

As long ago as 1830 (*d*), the doctrine was approved that a father, even under Mitakshara law, can, without the assent of his son, aliene a small portion of the ancestral property for pious purposes, which were specified to be the performance of ancestral rites, and the support of Brahmins and priests. The law does not favour endowment to the extent of enabling an owner to dispense with any fetters on his power of alienation. A widow, for example, cannot endow, at least in Bengal, without the consent of the reversioners, however beneficial such dedication may be deemed to be to her deceased husband's soul.

As soon as land or other property has been validly dedicated and assigned to the support of religion, the donor ceases to have any right in it (*e*); it is no longer heritable by his heirs, and he

(*a*) Mahatabchand and others *v.* Mirdad Ali and others, 5 S. D. R. p. 268.

(*b*) Mudden Lall *v.* Sreemutty Komul Bibee, 8 S. W. R., p. 43.

(*c*) Reg. XIX. of 1793, Sec. 2; Collector of Moorshedabad *v.* Bishennath Rai and others, Select Reports (new edition), Vol. I., p. 231.

(*d*) Gopalchunder Pande *v.* Babu Kunwar Singh, 5 S. D. A., p. 28; and see Raghunath *v.* Gobind Prasad I. L. R. 8 All. 76.

(*e*) 2 Macnaghten's Hindu Law, 305, case xiii.

cannot aliene it. Lands, which are held by a zemindar for a religious appropriation, even though he retains the superintendence, are not considered to form part of his zemindari, nor to be the subject of his ownership. The management of such land passes to the Sebait of the idol, or the mohunt of the temple, as the case may be, who can neither aliene it nor grant a pottah (*a*) of it, except for the term of his own life.

Subject to any usage to the contrary, the right to such management passes by inheritance. In Bengal, however, the succession to the superintendence of *muths*, or temples, is generally elective (*b*).

Such grants are not invalid either as gifts to superstitious uses or as creating perpetuities. A gift to an idol being valid by Hindu law, does not become invalid by reason of the English rule against perpetuities (*c*).

Such grants must be *bonâ fide* and not colourable, if they are to be upheld by the Courts. When the donor reserves to himself and family the direction and superintendence of the religious establishment, it is necessary to show, before the lands can be claimed as dewutter, that the proceeds (*d*) have been *bonâ fide* appropriated to religious purposes, and so long as that is done there is no objection to the donor retaining to himself and his family the management, receiving the rents and appointing the various officers who perform the worship. He then holds, not in his character of owner, but as Sebait, and in that capacity his power of alienation is gone (*e*). His competency extends no further than to the superintendence of the worship of the idols and to the payment of revenue to Govern-

(*a*) Radha Bullubh Chund *v.* Juggutchunder Chowdry, Select Reports (new edition), Vol. IV., p. 192.

(*b*) 1 Strange's Hindu Law, p. 151.

(*c*) Kumara Asima *v.* Kumara Krishna, 2 B. L. R., O. C. J., 47.

(*d*) Collector of Moorshedabad *v.* Bishennath Rai. Sel. Rep. (new edition), Vol. I., p. 231.

(*e*) Bhowanipershad Chowdhree *v.* Ranee Jagadumba, Ibid., Vol. I., 437.

ment; and perhaps to granting a pottah for the term of his own life.

Although dewutter lands cannot be either partitioned or aliened, the heirs of the grantor for whose benefit the worship is conducted can, by consent, form separate religious establishments, and separately perform the services; each one taking a separate share of the rents for that purpose, or taking the whole for his proportionate part of the year, or for any other space of time which may be agreed on between the parties for their *pallas*, or turns of worship. Obstruction to the use and worship of an idol by one joint worshipper is ground for the other insisting upon a separation and a removal of the idol to his house.

The devolution of the trust, on the death of the trustee, must depend on the terms of the trust deed, or the usage of each particular institution. "If a person," said Sir Barnes Peacock, "endows a college or religious institution, the endower has a right to lay down the rule of succession. But when no such rule is laid down, it must be proved by evidence what is the usage, in order to carry out the intention of the original endower. Each case must be governed by the usage of the particular mohuntee" (*a*). If there is no evidence of usage, the Sebaitship or trusteeship will pass to the heirs of the original donee, and the property will pass with it; while the founder and his heirs, in the absence of any express reservation in the deed, will have no power of supervision, removal or nomination, greater than any private person interested in the trust. In default of any trustee being appointed, as soon as the worship of a Thakoor has been founded, the Sebaitship vests in the founder and his heirs (*b*).

The general superintendence of endowments was originally vested in the Board of Revenue by Regulation XIX. of 1810. The Act XX. of 1863 is now the governing enactment.

(*a*) Greedharee Doss *v.* Nundkishore Dutt Mohunt, Marshall's Rep. p. 573, affirmed 11 Moore I. A., 428. See Janoki *v.* Gopal, L. R. 10 I. A., 32, 37.

(*b*) Gossamee *v.* Rumanlolljee, L. R., 16 I. A., 137.

CHAPTER XIII.

THE RITE AND CONTRACT OF ADOPTION.

Motives for adoption—Dattaka adoption—Kritrima form—Mode of effecting a dattaka adoption—No ceremonies necessary amongst Sudras—Ceremonies amongst the three higher castes—Datta homam—Effect of its omission—Evidence of adoption.

ADOPTION is a subject of great legal importance, owing to its effect on the devolution of property. The essential element of its best known form is the entire separation of a child from his family of birth and his entire absorption into another. Like all the rules of succession, the practice of adoption was originally based on religious principles. In the earliest times, *puttra* was the name given to a son by Brahma himself, because he delivered his father from the region of torment named *put;* and the idea of a departed spirit being refused admission to heaven because he had left no male issue was forcibly impressed upon the national mind by the earlier sages. A further theory existed from the most primitive times, viz., that by the eldest son at the moment of birth, the father discharged his debt to his own progenitors (*a*); and was by reason of that birth, irrespectively of his son surviving him, relieved from some of his liabilities in the future world. By Sancha and Lichita, it was said that a man became entitled to heaven by the birth of his son, and was exonerated through his oblation of funeral cakes from debt to his progenitors, and that the perpetual support of a consecrated fire and other observances did not procure a

(*a*) 9 Menu, verse 100.—By the eldest, at the moment of his birth, the father having begotten a son discharges his debt to his own progenitors.

sixteenth part of the benefit which arose from the birth of the eldest son. And Menu, in describing the sons who are substituted for sons of the body, says (*a*) that they are allowed by wise legislators for the sake of preventing a failure of obsequies.

Thus far the idea seems to be that the son delivers the father from torment through the funeral obsequies. But Menu himself, as well as all the other sages, directs by whom the obsequies are to be performed in the absence of sons; devolving the duty upon kinsmen in regular gradation, declaring that, on failure of all these, certain Brahmanas must offer the cake, and thus he says the rites of obsequies cannot fail (*b*). Here, therefore, the supreme necessity for a son seems to be lost sight of for every care is taken that the ancestor should, in any case, be provided with the funeral cake. The author (*c*) of the Dattaka Mimansa distinctly abandons the theory of a son's performance of obsequies being necessary simply for the purpose of delivering from *put*, and substitutes for it the notion that it is essential merely for the acquisition of some particular heaven, which is not to be acquired by such rites as are executed by the wife and the rest. He does not, therefore, refer the duty of adoption to the desire to be delivered from *put;* but quoting again from Menu, he says that a son must be anxiously desired for the sake of the funeral cake, water, and solemn rites, and *for the celebrity of his name.* (Sect. I., v. 9.)

In the Dattaka Chandrika (*d*) also, the preservation and continuance of the lineage are insisted upon as the chief objects of affiliation. At the present day its chief object is to effect the devolution of property.

(*a*) Colebrooke's Digest, Book V., Chap. IV., Sect. XV., verse 301.

(*b*) Colebrooke's Digest, Book V., Chap. VIII., Sect. I., verse 442. Menu—On failure of all those (natural heirs) the legal heirs are such Brahmanas as have read the three Vedas, as are pure in body and mind, as have subdued their passions, and they must consequently offer the cake: thus the rites of obsequies cannot fail.

(*c*) Dattaka Mimansa, Sect. I., verses 58, 59.

(*d*) Dattaka Chandrika, Sect. I., verses 25, 26.

Menu enumerated twelve different classes of sons (*a*), but of these the son by birth and the son by adoption, either by the Dattaka or Kritrima form, alone remain. The Dattaka adoption alone is prevalent in Bengal and most parts of India. The Kritrima adoption prevails in the Mithila country, and is rarely practised elsewhere. There are, besides, many forms of adoption peculiar to different localities, and mostly of a secular character. The Dattaka form effects a complete and irrevocable transfer of a child from one family to another, severing the tie to the natural parents and kindred as thoroughly as nature will permit, and creating a link to the adoptive family as firm as that created by actual birth in it. When once this form is completed, it can never be revoked. The adopted son cannot return to his natural family, nor can he be deprived of membership of the family to which he has been transferred, for any reasons short of those which would suffice to render a natural born son an outcast, or deprive him of his right of inheritance. He loses all claim to the property of his natural family, and all rights which would have accrued to him from belonging to it; but the prohibited degrees continue in full force; and for purposes of marriage and mourning and the days of impurity he remains affected by the former tie. The Kritrima form was a local innovation on the Dattaka form, and differs widely therefrom. It has no connection with religious ideas—is wholly non-Brahminical. The *kritrima* adopted son does not lose his claim to his own family, or his rights of inheritance therein. He does not even take the name of his adoptive father, but he succeeds to his estate and performs his obsequies, although he does not continue in the family. Such an adoption is a merely temporary arrangement, one which exists between the individual parties to the transaction and does not extend beyond them. A son so obtained is not initiated in any rites in the family of

(*a*) Menu IX., vv. 158—160.

his adoptive parent, nor does he assume any relationship whatever to the adopter's father. No ceremony is required, and the adoption is instantaneously perfected by the offer of adopting and the consent of the adopted party. A husband may adopt one *kritrima* son, and the wife another.

The mode of effecting a Dattaka adoption, which is generally of a child whose consent is from his age out of the question, is important. The essential operative part of the ceremony is the actual gift and acceptance of a child manifested by some overt act, that is, bodily transfer. The earliest European authorities so held (*a*), and the Privy Council has so decided (*b*) in a case between Sudras. It is necessary to draw special attention to this that the Courts insist upon an actual bodily transfer of the child being proved, and altogether refuse to recognise anything in the nature of a constructive giving and taking. The ceremony of gift must be not merely a form; it must be a fact patent to all beholders, the natural parent in person must actually with his own hand transfer the body of the child to the adoptive parent in person.

Again, in the case of Srinarayan Mitter *v.* Srimati Krishna Soondari Dassee (*c*), it was contended that the execution of two deeds of agreement to give and receive a child in adoption amounted to an actual giving and acceptance of the child, and constituted a valid adoption. But the Court held that the execution of the two deeds did not amount to an actual transfer, and that even the change of name supposed to be evidenced by the deed was not a sufficiently overt act to show that the child was given or received.

(*a*) See Strange's Hindu Law, Vol. I., c. 4, p. 94; Macnaghten's Hindu Law, p. 69, note. Mr. Ellis in Strange's Hindu Law, Vol. II., p. 87.

(*b*) Mahashoya Shosimath *v.* Srimati Krishna, L. R. 7, I. A., 250. See also p. 24.

(*c*) Siddessorry Dossee *v.* Doorgachurn Doss, 2 Ind. Jur., N.S., p. 22; 2 Bengal Law Reports, A. C., p. 279.

No ceremonies are necessary amongst Sudras; actual delivery of the child is: and where deeds of gift and acceptance had been executed and registered, it was held ineffectual without delivery (*a*). With regard to the three higher castes there is considerable difference of opinion as to the necessity for religious ceremonies; and their absence is very material, at all events as throwing light on the question whether there was any real intention to effect an adoption. Assuming such intention to be clear, the controversy seems to centre round the datta homam, or sacrifice to fire. The Madras High Court in the case of V. Singamma and V. Venkatacharlu (*b*) decided in the negative, that the datta homam was not necessary even amongst Brahmins. It said:—"In the two celebrated treatises on adoption, *viz.*, the Dattaka Mimansa and the Dattaka Chandrika, the observance of the prescribed solemnities (including a burnt sacrifice and recitation of the prayers denominated *Vyakrit*) is certainly treated as essential to the validity of the adoption, and to the establishment of the filial relation, in the case at all events of the son given. But the writers of these treatises depend mainly upon the texts of Vaṣishta and Saunaka as the authorities for their position, and these texts enjoin in similar terms the observance of various other solemnities on the occasion of an adoption, some of which appear not to be regarded as essential by the commentator." The Madras High Court then passed in review the opinion of Jagannatha, who, however, is of no authority in that part of India; of Sir Thomas Strange, expressed in his judgment in Veerapermal Pillay *v.* Naraina Pillay and in his work on Hindu law; the opinions of Mr. Colebrooke and Mr. Ellis; and the dictum of Lord Wynford (*c*)—"neither written acknowledgments nor the performance of any religious ceremonial are essential to the validity

(*a*) Mahashoya Shosimath *v.* Srimati Krishna, L. R. 7, I. A., 250. See also p. 24.

(*b*) 4 Mad. H. C., 165.

(*c*) See Sutroogun Sutputty *v.* Sabitr Dye, 2 Knapp P. C., 290.

of adoption." The High Court further considered that view of the case to be more consistent with its own previous decisions. This ruling was also affirmed by the same Court in a case between Kshatriyas (*a*).

There is, however, a considerable amount of authority to the contrary. In Bhairabnath Sye *v.* Maheshchunder Bhadury (*b*), which was a case between Sudras, the High Court referred to the opinions of Strange and Ellis, and considered that the law there laid down had been successfully attacked by Baboo Shamachurn Sircar in his Vyavastha Darpana (*c*); and that the passages from the Dattaka Mimansa and Dattaka Chandrika, on which he relied, show that Sir Thomas Strange's rule is incorrect, when he says that all that is legally necessary for an adoption is "gift and acceptance manifested by some overt act;" for that the filial relation is authoritatively stated to fail if either gift, acceptance, sacrifice, or so forth, as described in the fifth section of the Dattaka Mimansa (*d*), should be wanting. The Court also, upon the authority of Baboo Shamachurn Sircar, held that Sudras could employ Brahmins to perform the rite of the datta homam for them, and that the performance of it was necessary also in their case for a valid adoption.

So far as this case is an authority that the datta homam ceremony is essential to adoption amongst Sudras it has been overruled by the Privy Council (*e*). So far as it prescribes the datta homam as essential to the validity of adoption amongst the three higher castes, there is a dictum of the Privy Council to the effect that "certain religious ceremonies, the datta homam in particular, are in this case requisite" (*f*).

(*a*) Chandramala *v.* Muktamala, I. L. R., 6 Mad., 20.

(*b*) 4 Beng. L. R. (A. C. J.), 162, and see 5 B. L. R., 366.

(*c*) P. 874.

(*d*) Dattaka Mimansa, Chap. V., verses 45, 46, and 56.

(*e*) Indromoni Chowdhani *v.* Behari Lal Mullick, I. L. R. 7 I. A., 24.

(*f*) Mahashoya Shosimath *v.* Srimati Krishna, L. R. 7, I. A., 256.

The Madras High Court relying on this dictum (*a*) doubted their former ruling, and held the datta homam to be unnecessary only in the exceptional case of the adoption being of a brother's son, the parties thus being all of the same gotra. In Bombay and Allahabad (*b*) the same ruling has been confined to the case of a brother's son having been adopted. And it must be taken that as regards adoption from a different gotra the balance of authority at the present time is in favour of the datta homam being an essential part of the ceremony as regards the three higher castes, and in the absence of a proved usage to the contrary.

Assuming the datta homam to be an essential portion of a valid adoption amongst the three higher castes, it does not necessarily follow that an adoption made and acted upon will be set aside merely because that ceremony has been omitted. The rule is directory, and an adoption ought not to take place in disregard of it; but the rule is not prohibitive, so as to vitiate such adoption absolutely and completely. On the contrary the maxim *Factum valet quod fieri non debuit* may be applied and is recognised as applicable both by the High Courts of Bombay and Allahabad (*c*).

With regard to the evidence of adoption, according to Hindu law, neither registration of the act of adoption, nor any written evidence of that act, nor any written evidence of the grant of an authority in that behalf, when such act is done in pursuance of authority, nor the sanction of any Court of Justice or any ruling power, is essential to its validity. It may be proved by verbal testimony, at any distance of time, after it is supposed to have taken place, and it may take place even fifty years after the adoptive father's death, in

(*a*) See I. L. R. 11 Mad., 5, and 13 Mad., 214.

(*b*) I. L. R. 11 Bomb., 381, and I. L. R. 6 All., 276.

(*c*) See I. L. R. 10 Bomb., 86, and I. L. R. 9 All., 253.

pursuance of an authority ascertained to have been given by him, which authority itself may also be proved by parol evidence.

But, although neither registration, nor written acknowledgments, nor attested agreements are essential to the validity of adoption, nevertheless the utmost publicity is usual, and its absence suspicious. The ceremonial observed at the time, the assembling of the members of the family and their friends, and the notice which is frequently given to the ruling power, guarantee the genuineness of the act; and there is this further security, that some of the most important ceremonies of regeneration ought to be performed upon the child in the name and family of his adoptive father. Although they might be neglected, it is scarcely probable that they would be so in the case of a *bonâ fide* adoption.

Where some time has elapsed, evidence of repute like that which is relied on in cases of marriage and legitimacy would be admissible. But the ruling of the Privy Council (*a*) that a suit to set aside an adoption cannot be brought, nor any suit to recover possession of property founded on such invalidity, more than twelve years after its performance prevents an adoption being brought into question after such lapse of time as to render suitable evidence unprocurable.

(*a*) Jagadamba Chowdhrani *v.* Dakhina Mohun, L. R. 13 I. A., 84.

CHAPTER XIV.

Adoption.—Who May Adopt.

Who may adopt—Sonless men—Minors—Unmarried men—Impotent men—Disqualifications for adopting—Women—Wives and widows can adopt with the husband's consent—When a widow may adopt without husband's consent—Consent of husband's sapindas—Limits to widow's exercise of authority given by her husband—When the absence of such authority can be supplied—Right to adopt in Kritrima form.

A Hindu is subject to but few restrictions when he comes to exercise the right of adopting a son, and he is not fettered by any provisions of law introduced to secure the interests of any child whom he may wish to obtain. The law of adoption chiefly deals with the right to give a son, the right to receive him, and the eligibility of the child to secure to his adoptive parents the objects for which they received him in adoption. The circumstances which, on the one hand, give birth to those rights of giving and receiving, and on the other secure the objects in view, are somewhat complicated in their character, and require the closest attention; and thus the law relating to adoption, though nearly uniform throughout India, is one of some difficulty.

With respect to the first of these questions, as to the circumstances under which a right to adopt arises. On this subject, the general rule is in the words of Atri (*a*) that " by a man destitute of a son only, must a substitute for the same always be adopted; with some one resource for the sake of the funeral

(*a*) Dattaka Mimansa, sect. I., verse 3.

H

cake, water, and solemn rites." The rule is also given by Menu in very similar words.

It must be understood that the destitution referred to is at the time of the adoption. A man to whom no son has been born, or whose son has died, is within the meaning of the term *aputra*, and may adopt. The son referred to includes the son's son and son's grandson, for either of these is denoted by the term male issue (the absence of which is a bar to the entrance of heaven), and is capable of performing the funeral obsequies (*a*).

So long as no son exists a man is *aputra*. He need not wait till he is hopeless of issue. Even the pregnancy of his wife has been held not to prevent or delay adoption. In a Madras decision (*b*) to that effect it is said that otherwise an adoption might be prevented, not merely by his own wife's pregnancy, but by that of his son's or grandson's widow. Of course if he had either son or grandson living he would not be *aputra*, but the existence of an unborn male descendant does not prevent adoption.

With regard to other qualifications besides being *aputra* the main question is whether a minor can adopt. The shasters are silent on the subject. So far as adoption is a religious rite it would fall within the competence of a minor, so far as it is a civil act of the first importance, altering the devolution of property to the exclusion of those who claim by legal inheritance, it would *primâ facie* not be within his legal capacity. The question depends on statute law and judicial decision. Those minors who are under the Court of Wards are forbidden by the various Court of Wards' Acts to adopt without the consent of the Court. Where they apply, an adoption made in violation of them is absolutely invalid. The Privy Council (*c*), however,

(*a*) Dattaka Mimansa, Chap. I., verse 13.—By a man destitute of a son. The word "son" here used is inclusive also of the son's son and grandson, for through these the exclusion from heaven denounced in such passages as "Heaven awaits not one destitute of a son" is removed.

(*b*) Nagabushanam *v.* Seshammagaru, I. L. R. 3 Mad., 180.

(*c*) Jumoona *v.* Bamasoonderai, L. R. 3 I. A., 72.

has held that this disability only affects those who are under the actual guardianship of the Court of Wards. In the same case it appears to sanction the view that a valid authority to adopt can be granted by a Hindu minor who is not under the Court of Wards, but has attained to years of discretion according to the Hindu law. The Bengal and Bombay High Courts (*a*) extend this doctrine to the case of an actual adoption by a minor, provided he has attained years of discretion. The principle of such decisions is that the act is not void, and as it is not prejudicial to the minor's interests it is not voidable after he attains majority. When he attains years of discretion is not easy to determine.

With regard to unmarried men, they may adopt, for, as Jagannatha says, there is no law which forbids them. So also may a widower or a man who has forsaken his wife. There have been recent decisions to that effect (*b*).

An impotent man stands on the same footing as any other person disqualified from inheriting by any personal disabilities, such as leprosy or any other incurable disease, or blindness. The validity of any adoption made by him would depend upon his capacity to perform whatever religious ceremonies were necessary, either after expiation, penance, or otherwise. In Sayamalal Dutt *v.* Saudamini (*c*) a widow's unchastity was held to invalidate any adoption made by her, for it unfitted her to take part in any religious ceremony.

There are two cases given in the second volume of Macnaghten's Hindu Law (*d*), in one of which it was decided that a person afflicted with leprosy is incapable of adopting, and in the other that, if he has performed the prescribed penances, that

(*a*) Rajendro Narain *v.* Saroda, 15 S. W. R., 548. Patel Vandravan *v.* Patel Manital, I. L. R. 15 Bomb., 565.

(*b*) Gopal Anant *v.* Narayan, I. L. R. 12 Bomb., 329; Tulshi Ram *v.* Behari Lal, I. L. R. 12 All., 352.

(*c*) 5 Beng. L. R., 362.

(*d*) See Volume II., page 201, cases xx. and xxi.

incapacity is removed. Expiation is said to be necessary to enable a polluted person to perform the religious acts ordained in the Vedas. And before the Privy Council (*a*) it seems to have been taken as admitted law that adoption by a person while under pollution in consequence of the death of a relation would be invalid.

As between husband and wife an adoption is always to the husband and for his benefit; accordingly his right to adopt is absolute. It is never dependent on her consent (*b*), on the contrary he is competent to effect it notwithstanding her dissent. By his individual act of adoption he can affiliate a child both to himself and his wife.

Next comes the question of the legal capacity of a woman to adopt a son. Upon this subject, with regard to adoption in the ordinary and full meaning of the term,—that is, adoption in the *dattaka* form, the text of Vasishta (*c*)—" Let not a woman either give or receive a son, unless with the assent of her husband " declares a prohibition, which is in full force at the present day. The rule of law may be laid down that a woman, whether wife or widow, is unable to adopt a son in the *dattaka* form as son to herself exclusively. In either capacity her only power to adopt is a vicarious one—a power to adopt a son to her husband, who *ipso facto* becomes a son to herself. The wife must always have her husband's assent before adopting in the *dattaka* form. With regard to widows there are four different rules all grounded on the above text of Vasishta. According to the Bengal school and the Benares school as prevailing in Upper India, there must have been an express authority given by the husband, to take effect after his death; which authority must be strictly followed, for it is the sole source of the widow's power. It may be given orally, but in

(*a*) Ramalinga Pillai *v.* Sudasiva Pillai, 1 S. W. R., P.C., page 25.

(*b*) Alank Munjari *v.* Fakir Chand Sirkar, 5 S. D. A., 356.

(*c*) Colebrooke's Digest, Bk. V., Chap. IV., s. 8, v. 273.

that case must be clearly proved; or by writing; or by *onomutteeputtre* or will. It may be given to be exercised contingently on the happening of some event, *e.g.*, the death of sons; but it can only be exercised in such circumstances as would have authorised the husband if living to adopt.

According to the Mahratta school which governs Western India, the text of Vasishta only applies to adoptions made in the husband's lifetime. Accordingly a wife must have her husband's consent before adopting, but the widow who is no longer able to obtain her husband's consent may nevertheless adopt, since her act is beneficial to her husband's soul (*a*); unless he has forbidden it.

According to the Mithila school the assent of the husband must be given at the time of adopting, and consequently a widow cannot in the Mithila country adopt at all in the *dattaka* form. But as the Kritrima form prevails in that part of India, the rule has very little practical application.

According to the Dravida school, which prevails in Southern India, the widow should have her husband's authority; but if it has not been obtained, the want of it may be supplied by her husband's kinsmen or sapindas.

Under these circumstances the two practical subjects to be considered are, what are the limits to the exercise of the authority to adopt when the husband has given it; and when he has not given it, within what limits it may be supplied.

First, with regard to the widow's exercise of an authority duly given by her husband. She is not disqualified by minority, for the civil act is her husband's, and she is only the instrument for carrying into effect his wishes (*b*). Incapacity to perform religious ceremonies, where these are necessary, would disqualify her; *e.g.*, unchastity. On the other hand, no disqualification on her part would suffice to enlarge the power

(*a*) Collector of Madura *v.* Mootoo Ramalinga, 12 Moore, I. A., 436.
(*b*) Mondakini *v.* Adinath, I. L. R. 18 Cal., 69.

either of the husband or the sapindas (where their assent may supply the absence of his) to give to any one but the widow authority to adopt. Such authority cannot under any circumstances be delegated to any one else. Moreover, the widow cannot be compelled to act upon it; it is at her option whether and when she will do so, and if she choose to hold it without exercising it till nearly the close of her life, there are no means of preventing her (*a*).

It may be convenient here to point out that the widow who is thus supposed to receive from her husband a power to adopt, has nearly always a direct interest opposed to the adoption, leading her to refuse or to delay the execution of the power which is conferred upon her solely for the purpose of fulfilling the wishes and advancing the interests of her husband.

Take for instance the case of every Hindu widow in Bengal, and of those widows in the wide provinces subject to Mitakshara law, whose husbands were without brothers or were separated from them. Failing male issue, or otherwise the power to adopt could not be exercised by them, the widows are entitled to succeed to the whole of their husbands' estates and to possess and enjoy them till their deaths. But the moment a widow exercises the power and adopts a son, she is *ipso facto* divested of the whole of the estate, which immediately devolves upon the child. As stated by the Privy Council, in (*b*) *Dhurmadoss Panday* v. *Mussamut Shama Soondry Debiah*, the result of an act of adoption by a Hindu widow is, that the whole property is divested from her, and vested in the adopted son. She stands to the estate from that moment simply in the relation of guardian of her son, bound to deliver over possession to him on his attaining the age of majority, and accountable to him for every act which she does in reference to it. Her interest in it is cut down to the widow's right to

(*a*) Bamandoss *v*. Mt. Tarinee, 7 Moore, I. A., 190.
(*b*) 3 Moore, I. A., 242.

maintenance, which is no doubt a primary charge upon it, but may bear a comparatively small proportion to its extent and value. The possession of the power to adopt involves no legal duty, and does not, so long as it is not exercised, affect in the slightest degree the interest which the widow takes. In one point of view it enables her to devote herself to the future welfare of her husband, by providing him with the advantages of sonship; on the other it arms her with a weapon against his reversionary heirs, with which she may at any moment exclude them from the inheritance.

The case (*a*) of *Bamandoss Mookerjee* v. *Mussamut Tarinee*, decided by the Privy Council in 1858, is the leading authority for the proposition that the mere fact of a Hindu widow omitting or refusing to exercise the permission to adopt given to her by her husband does not affect her heritable right. Before she adopts, she takes her husband's estate as heiress, and she is entitled to retain it in that capacity until she chooses by her voluntary act of adoption to divest herself of it. The devolution of the estate upon a Hindu widow is not affected in the least degree by a power of adoption being given and by the possibility of a third person coming into existence with the superior title of adopted son.

There is an important limitation upon her authority connected with her title to her husband's estate. If, for instance, that is gone by reason of her husband having predeceased his son; then on the death of the latter sonless, in which case alone could her power to adopt arise, the son's widow would take the estate as the son's heiress. The Privy Council has decided that upon the vesting of the husband's estate in the son's widow, the power of adoption granted by the husband is at an end and incapable of execution. Even if it were capable of being acted upon, an adoption by the mother-in-law could not operate

(*a*) 7 Moore, I. A., 169.

to divest the daughter-in-law of her estate. That could only be done by the daughter-in-law adopting to her deceased husband in pursuance of an authority validly granted by him. Bhoobunmoye *v.* Ram Kishore Achari (*a*) is the authority for this doctrine, which has ever since been implicitly followed. The following passage of the judgment is important:—

"The question is whether the estate of Gourkishore's son being unlimited, that son having married and left a widow his heir, and that heir having acquired a vested estate in her husband's property as widow, a new heir can be substituted by adoption who is to defeat that estate, and take as an adopted son what a legitimate son of Gourkishore would not have taken. This seems contrary to all reason and to all the principles of Hindu law as far as we can collect them. . . . No case has been produced, no decision has been cited from the text books, and no principle has been stated to show that by the mere gift of a power of adoption to a widow the estate of the heir of the deceased son vested in possession can be defeated and devested."

Their Lordships held that the power to adopt given by Gourkishore was at an end.

If the son in that case had not left a widow and the estate had gone to his mother as his heiress she could then have exercised the power of adoption given to her by Gourkishore (*b*).

Next with regard to supplying in Southern India the absence of the husband's authority by the consent of his kindred; the Privy Council decision in Collector of Madura *v.* Ramalinga Sathupatty (*c*), called the Ramnad case, is the governing authority. There the High Court found that an adoption had been made by the widow with the assent of the majority of her husband's *sapindas*. The Privy Council treated it as

(*a*) 10 Moore, I. A., 279, 311, and see also L. R. 8 I. A., 229; 14 I. A., 67; 16 I. A., 166.

(*b*) Rajah Vellanki *v.* Venkata Rama, L. R., 4 I. A., 1.

(*c*) 12 Moore, I. A., 440.

an admitted proposition that a widow has the power to receive a son in adoption to her husband according to all the schools of Hindu law, except that of Mithila; but that such power is subject to conditions. According to the Bengal school it is established beyond all doubt that she must have the formal permission of her husband, given in his lifetime, verbally or in writing, but clearly proved. Other schools extend the right of the widow to adopt to cases where, although the husband has abstained from giving his permission, his kindred, after his death, *bonâ fide* authorise or consent to the act. The point in dispute was, whether the doctrine of the assent of the husband's kindred being of sufficient authority to the widow, was limited to the Mahratta school in which the treatise called the Mayukha is the predominant authority; or whether it was common to the followers of the Mitakshara in the Benares, as well as in the Mahratta school, and as such to be receivable as the law current in Vizagapatam, where the litigation had arisen. Balambhatta, who was a commentator of the Benares school, contends that a woman's right of adopting, as well as of giving, a son is common to the widow and to the wife, and does not enforce the usual restrictions; and Mr. Colebrooke's note to the Mitakshara (*a*), and several notes of his in the second volume of Strange's Hindu Law, were quoted to show that, according to his opinion, all the followers of the Mitakshara, whether of the Benares or of the Mahratta school, recognised a widow's adoption when made with the consent of her husband's kindred. The Privy Council also cited and approved the following statement of the law by Sir Thomas Strange: (*b*) "Equally loose is the reason alleged against adoption by a widow, since the assent of the husband may be given to take effect like a will after his death; and according to the doctrine of the Benares and Mahratta schools prevailing in the peninsula, it may be

(*a*) Mitakshara, Chap. I., sec. XI., verse 9.

(*b*) Strange's Hindu Law, vol. I., p. 179.

supplied by that of his kindred, her natural guardians; but it is otherwise by the law that governs the Bengal Provinces."

And the further question disposed of by their lordships which appears to be all that was necessary to complete the rule of law upon this subject was, who are the kinsmen whose assent will supply the want of positive authority from the deceased husband in the provinces, where such want of authority may be supplied at all? When the husband's family is undivided, then it was said that under the law of the schools which admit this disputed power of adoption the father of the widow's deceased husband, if living, or at least the surviving brothers, who in default of adoption would take the husband's share, would obviously be the persons whose consent would be necessary; inasmuch as it would be unjust to allow the widow to defeat their interests by introducing a new coparcener against their will; the widow, according to those schools, not herself succeeding to a share of the joint estate. When, however, as in the case before the Council, the deceased husband was separate in estate, the widow takes it by inheritance, and then there is greater difficulty in laying down a rule. The reason, however, for the necessity of the assent of kinsmen, being the presumed incapacity of women for independence, rather than the necessity of procuring the consent of all those whose possible and reversionary interest in the estate would be defeated by the adoption, their lordships held that the consent of every kinsman was not essential. While ruling that every case must depend upon the circumstances of the family, their lordships laid it down that there should be such evidence of the assent of kinsmen as suffices to show that the act is done by the widow in the proper and *bona fide* performance of a religious duty, and neither capriciously nor from a corrupt motive.

Further, their lordships pointed out that, inasmuch as the authorities in favour of the widow's power to adopt, with the assent of her husband's kinsmen, proceed in a great measure upon the assumption that his assent to this meritorious act is to be implied wherever he has not forbidden it; so the power cannot be inferred when a prohibition by the husband either has been directly expressed by him or can be reasonably deduced from his disposition of his property, or from the existence of a direct line competent to the full performance of religious duties, or from the other circumstances of his family which afford no plea for a supercession of heirs on the ground of religious obligation in order to complete or fulfil defective religious rites.

A later case (*a*) affirmed an adoption on evidence that there had been a sufficient assent on the part of kinsmen to show that the act of adoption was done by the widow in the proper and *bonâ fide* performance of a religious duty. The Privy Council refused to examine the motives of the widow for adopting so long as they were neither corrupt nor capricious. Where the assent given was only of one separated and distant sapinda, himself the father of the adopted child, it was pointed out (*b*) that that was insufficient to authorise an adoption, which, however, appeared to be valid, since the husband's authority was proved. Otherwise the requisite authority in the case of an undivided family is to be sought within the family, even though the particular property devolving upon the adopted son is to be held in severalty and not in coparcenary.

With regard to the right to adopt in the kritrima form, which only exists in the Mithila country; having regard to its peculiar characteristics, that it effects no change of gotra, and is a mere temporary arrangement between two contracting parties, the capacity to receive a kritrima son is co-extensive with the capacity to contract. A widow cannot adopt to her husband, even if he has given her authority so to do, in that district. She can adopt to herself either during her husband's life or after his death (*c*).

(*a*) L. R. 4 I. A., 1.
(*b*) Sri Raghunada *v.* Sri Brozo Kishoro, L. R. 3 I. A., 154.
(*c* Shibo Koeree *v.* Joogun Singh, 8 S. W. R., 155.

CHAPTER XV.

ADOPTION.—WHO MAY BE ADOPTED.

Who may give in adoption—In kritrima form—In dattaka form—Father's power absolute—When mother may give—Only natural parents can give—Qualifications of child—Neither an only nor eldest son can be given—His natural mother must not stand to the adoptive father in the prohibited degrees of affinity—One of a different tribe or caste cannot be adopted—A sapinda should be selected, the nearer being preferred to the more remote—Age of the adopted child—Whether tonsure or upanayana having been performed is a bar to adoption.

THE question of who may be adopted relates to the power of a Hindu parent to give away a child and to the qualifications of the child necessary to render him eligible. Only such child can be received whose parent is entitled to part with him, and who is himself qualified to assume the relationship of a son in the family to which he is transferred.

In the *kritrima* form of adoption, to which in general the only parties are the adopter and the adopted, the assent of the person adopted is necessary if he has attained his majority, which consent must be given in the lifetime of the adopter (*a*). But where he is a minor, and therefore unable legally to give or express consent, the competence or legal ability to consent for him, and in effect to give him in adoption (*b*), would vest in one or both of his parents, unless he has been abandoned by his parents, in which case he can himself consent so as to make the adoption good.

(*a*) Durgopal Singh *v.* Roopun Singh, 6 S. D. R., 271. Musst Sutputtee *v.* Indranund, 2 Sel rep. 173.

(*b*) Sutherland's Synopsis, Note 8, 19. Menu, c. IX., verse 177.

Now as to the capacity to give a child in the *dattaka* form of adoption. According to Menu (*a*), a father has absolute power to give, the mother being only able to do so with her husband's consent. Balambhatta, however, says that three cases are provided for with reference to the right to give a child in adoption (*b*); and apparently his doctrine is that, although the right to receive in adoption is, as between the husband and wife, absolute in the husband, it does not follow that he can assert the same superiority over his wife in respect of giving away the child, which equally belongs to them both; but can only give away their child without her consent, if she be dead, insane, or otherwise incapable, unless the distress is very urgent. But besides the authority of Menu, for the father's absolute power in that respect, there is the direct authority of the Dattaka Mimansa, and the absence of any prohibition in the Dattaka Chandrika (*c*). The first rule then is that the father has absolute power to give away his son, provided that he has more than one, without the consent of the mother (*d*).

With regard to the mother's power to give, that appears from the text of Menu referred to above to be dependent upon her husband's consent. Vasishta (*e*) also ordained that a woman should neither give nor receive in adoption, unless

(*a*) 9 Menu, verse 168:—"He whom his father, or mother *with her husband's assent*, gives to another as his son, provided that the donee have no issue, if the boy be of the same class and affectionately disposed, is considered as a son given, the gift being confirmed by pouring water."

(*b*) Mitakshara, Chap. I., sec. XI., verse 9, *note*.

(*c*) Dattaka Mimansa, sec. IV., verse 13:—"The husband singly even and independent of his wife is competent to give a son."

Dattaka Chandrika, section I., verses 31, 32.—"But by a woman the gift may be made with her husband's sanction, if he be alive; or even without it, if he be dead, have emigrated, or entered a religious order." Accordingly Vasishta: "Let not a woman either give or receive a son, unless with the assent of her husband."

(*d*) This has been decided. See Chitko Rughanath *v.* Janaki, 11 Bomb. H. C., 199.

(*e*) Dattaka Mimansa, section I., verse 15. See also Mitakshara, Chap. I., section XI., verse 9.

with the consent of her husband. The consent, however, may be dispensed with when the husband is incapable of consenting (*a*), and has not prohibited it (*b*). And according to the Dattaka Mimansa, an exception is also made in case of urgent distress: "during a season of calamity" the widow may give away her son, even though it be impossible to obtain the assent of her husband.

The decided cases upon this point are not numerous. In Debee Dial *v.* Hur Hor Singh (4 Sel. rep. 320) where a widow had given away her son without her husband's consent or prohibition, the Court held it to be void *ab initio* even after a long recognition of him by the adoptive family as a son duly affiliated. One ground of objection was that he was an only son. But it was ruled, in accordance with the statement of the Pundits, that there is no precept in the shasters which enables a woman to give her son, even as a *dwyamushyayana,* or son of two fathers, without authority from her husband. On that ground alone it was held the adoption was void.

In spite of this case Mr. Sutherland's statement of the law will probably be accepted as correct. He says, in his Synopsis, that the true doctrine to be extracted from the opinions of the sages is (1) that the father may give away his minor son without the consent of the mother, though it is more laudable that he should consult her wishes; (2) that the mother generally is incapable of such gift while the father lives except in case of urgent distress and necessity; and (3) that she may do so upon her husband's death, also in case of urgent distress and necessity, emigration, entering a religious order, becoming an outcast, or being otherwise civilly dead.

The limitation upon such authority apparently is that it cannot be exercised in a manner of which the husband, if living, might have reasonably disapproved (*c*).

(*a*) Rangubai *v.* Bhagirthibai, I. L. R. 2 Bomb., 377, 380.

(*b*) Narayanasami *v.* Kuppusami, I. L. R. 11 Mad., 43.

(*c*) Laksmappa *v.* Ramava, 12 Bomb. H. C., 364; and see I. L. R. 6 Bomb., 524.

No one but the natural parents can give a child in adoption. The adoptive parents cannot do so, for in the first place an only son is ineligible for gift; and, in the second, such gift would be inconsistent with the terms of the contract on which such parents received the child, viz., "as a son to themselves." They can neither give such child away absolutely, nor can they give him as a *dwyamushyayana.*

Further, the brother cannot give in adoption even though both the natural parents be dead. Brothers stand upon an equality, one has no proprietary right in, or authority over, the person of another. It was so decided in the case of Mussamut Tarramonee Debea *v.* Deo Narayn Rai and Bishen Persad (*a*).

Further, the Madras High Court (*b*), in 1864, held that to constitute a valid adoption there must be a valid giving as well as receiving, and that where both parents are dead and there is no one to give the child, it cannot be received. No amount of ratification, it was said, can supply the essentials of such a transaction. That case over-ruled the decision in Verapermall Pillay *v.* Narain Pillay (*c*), where it was held that though both parents were dead a child might be given in adoption by his elder brother. Even a paternal grandfather cannot give his grandson in adoption (*d*). The parent alone can give, and he may lawfully impose conditions, the breach of which will avoid the adoption (*e*).

The effective limitations, however, to the capacity of the parents to give chiefly depend upon what they have got to give —that is to say, upon the qualifications of the child who is to be the subject of the gift. As to these there are four rules, three of them prohibitory and one directory. *First of all the*

(*a*) Select Reports (new edition), vol. III., p. 516.

(*b*) Subba Luvammai *v.* Ammakutti Ammal, 2 Mad. Rep., p. 129; and see 10 Bomb. H. C., 268.

(*c*) See Considerations of Hindu Law, pp. 186, 210.

(*d*) Collector of Surat *v.* Dhirsingji, 10 Bomb. H. C., 235.

(*e*) Rangubai *v.* Bhagirthibai, I. L. R. 2 Bomb., 377.

child must not be an only son, either natural or adopted, nor an eldest son. The early authorities are precise upon this point. Nanda Pandita (*a*) lays down the rule thus:—"He who has only one son is 'eka-putra,' or one having an only son; by such a one the gift of that son must not be made." Sancha (*b*) and Vasishta (*c*) are to the same effect. The reason is that the only son is destined to continue the line of his own ancestors. Mr. Sutherland says, and it is a generally accepted view, that an only son may be adopted as a *dwyamushyayana*, or son of two fathers. If a brother adopts a brother's only son that double relationship readily follows, in other cases a special contract would be necessary.

Then comes the question whether disregard of this prohibition renders the adoption of an only son void, or whether the principle *factum valet* applies. Upon that subject there was conflict of authority in 1870 between the different Presidencies (*d*), and it remains to the present day. The Madras (*e*) and Bombay High Courts (*f*) have held that such adoption, though in disregard of a religious prohibition, was not on that account legally invalid. But in Bengal, notwithstanding a case in Fulton's reports (*g*), relied upon by the Madras Court, the decisions have been the other way (*h*), that such an adoption is void. The adoption of an only son was placed on the same footing as an adoption by a widow without authority from her husband, and was ruled to be prohibited and void. The question at issue can now only be settled by a Privy Council decision.

(*a*) Dattaka Mimansa, s. IV., vv. 2 and 8.

(*b*) Dattaka Mimansa, s. IV., v. 3.

(*c*) Mitakshara, Chap. I., s. XI., v. 11.

(*d*) See Tagore Law Lectures, 1870, pp. 307 *et seq.*

(*e*) Chinna Gaundan *v.* Kumara Gaundan, 1 Mad. H. C., 54; I. L. R. 11 Mad., 43; and see Uma Deyi *v.* Gokoolanund, L. R. 5 I. A., 42.

(*f*) Nimbalha *v.* Banadir, 4 Bomb. A. C., 191.

(*g*) Joymony Dossee *v.* Sibosondry Dossee, Fulton, p. 75.

(*h*) Rajah Upendra Lal Roy *v.* Rani Prasannomayi, 1 B. L. R. A. C., 221; and see I. L. R. 3 Calc., 443.

But assuming that a man has no more power of gift over his only son than he has over his wife or any other relation, when does the right to give in adoption accrue? It appears that it properly arises only when the extinction of a man's own lineage is duly provided against. There is a precept in the Dattaka Mimansa (*a*) against the gift of one out of only two sons. That precept, however, is, in the language of Mr. Macnaghten (*b*), merely dissuasive, and not peremptory. Sir Thomas Strange (*c*) also says that, in strictness, it is not sufficient for a man to have more than one son before he gives in adoption; since, if having only two sons, he part with one, the death of the remaining one is not to be risked. This rule, however, is not of legal force, and accordingly if he have two he may relinquish the younger. The selection of the younger one should be made apparently in deference to the author of the Mitakshara, who forbids the gift of an eldest son, "for he chiefly fulfils the office of a son, as is shown in the following text, 'by the eldest son, as soon as born a man becomes the father of male issue.' The eldest son, therefore, as well as the only son, cannot be given in adoption except to a brother."

The Madras (*d*) High Court, however, have held that, even assuming the prohibition against an only son to be valid, it does not extend to invalidate the adoption of an eldest or only son of a brother.

The last surviving son is not regarded as an only son provided there be male issue living of the deceased sons. The father in that case is amply provided with male issue for all purposes, whether of performance of obsequies or of continuance of his lineage (*e*).

(*a*) Dattaka Mimansa, Chap. IV., v. 8.
(*b*) Principles of Hindu Law, p. 77.
(*c*) Strange's Hindu Law, vol. I., p. 85.
(*d*) Indian Jurist, O. S., p. 105.
(*e*) Macnaghten's Hindu Law, vol. I., p. 75.

Secondly, the child must be one whom his natural mother might have born to his adoptive father in a legal marriage, or whom his adoptive mother might have born to his natural father in a legal marriage. The son, therefore, of a sister or any other female relative of the adoptive father, with whom he could not have legally intermarried, cannot be affiliated by him. In the language of the text (*a*) "the boy must bear the reflection of a son," which is described to be the capability to have sprung from the adopter himself through an appointment to raise issue on another's wife. Accordingly the brother, paternal and maternal uncles, the daughter's son and that of the sister, are all excluded, for they are all unfitted to have been begotten by the individual himself through an appointment to raise issue on the wife of another.

The necessary inference from this doctrine is that any adoption which imports incest, that is, any child of a woman standing towards the adoptive father in the prohibited degrees of affinity, cannot be received by him. The principle of law which forbids it underlies the whole theory and practice of affiliation as it is understood amongst Hindus. Accordingly, there can be no question that the prohibition to adopt such a child (*b*), whether explicit or inferred, is one of positive and peremptory character, and is not to be viewed as merely dissuasive, or of a nature importing such merely religious obligations as would make a man only responsible for its breach either in *in foro conscientiæ* or to the spiritual authorities in the family or caste to which he belongs. In Bengal there was originally some hesitation in affirming this principle, and a Brahmin's adoption of a sister's son was in one instance declared to be valid. But in Sir Francis Macnaghten's Considerations of Hindu Law (*c*), a work which was first published

(*a*) Dattaka Mimansa, s. V., v. 16.

(*b*) See Dattaka Mimansa, s. II., v. 34; Dattaka Mimansa, s. V., v. 17; Dattaka Chandrika, s. I., v. 17.

(*c*) Considerations of Hindu Law, pp. 166, 174.

in 1824, there is a case referred to in which the Supreme Court recognised the invalidity of any adoption by a man (meaning of course of the three superior castes), of a child whom he could not have begotten on his natural mother without incest; and also affirmed the further rule that he cannot adopt a child as his, by a particular wife, nor can she after his death adopt to him a child whom she could not have borne without incest to his natural father. Natural relationship is the foundation of the rule. The change is both of paternity and also of maternity, and if either the one or the other imports a prohibited connection, it violates an essential principle of a Hindu adoption. The adoptive father and the natural mother must have been in point of affinity capable of contracting a legal marriage; and so also must have been the adoptive mother and the natural father.

This rule binds all Hindus of the three superior castes according to all the schools of Hindu law which admit the *dattaka* form of adoption; and it is applied in Madras, Bengal, and the North-West Provinces.

The authority on which it rests is given by the Madras High Court in the case of Narasammai *v.* Balara Macharlu (*a*); referring to Mr. Sutherland, who regarded it as a fundamental principle that the person to be adopted must be one with the mother of whom the adopter might have intermarried; to the passage in Strange (*b*), which forbids such adoption by one of the three higher classes and allows it to the Sudras; and to the Dattaka Chandrika, s. 2, par. 8, which defines the reflection of a son as " the capability to be begotten by the adopter through appointment and so forth."

Sudras have, however, always been excepted from this rule. Jats and Jains are also exempt from it, and where local custom is in favour of exemption effect will be given to it.

(*a*) 1 Mad. H. C., 420.

(*b*) Strange, vol. I., p. 84.

With regard to the law which prevails in the province of Mithila, that rests upon a different footing. The *kritrima* adoption effects no change either of paternity or maternity. The son so received is not transferred from one family to another. There is merely a temporary arrangement between the adopter and the adopted, with the addition of certain legal rights of inheritance and legal duties. Accordingly, a sister's son may be received in adoption without violating Hindu law as interpreted by the doctrines of the Mithila school. In the case of Chowdree Purmessur Dutt Jha *v.* Hunooman Dutt Ray (*a*), it was held that the rule in regard to a *dattaka* adoption which bars the adoption of a child of a mother within the prohibited degrees of marriage is not applicable to the *kritrima* adoption as practised in Mithila; referring to Ooman Dutt *v.* Kunhia Singh (*b*), where the same principle had been affirmed in reference to the daughter's son; and equality of caste was recognised as the only condition of eligibility for that mode of affiliation.

The third rule is that *one of a different class or tribe or caste cannot be adopted:* "should one of a different class be taken as a son in any instance, let the adopter not make him a participator of a share (*c*); this is the doctrine of Saunaka;" and the author of the Dattaka Mimansa also quotes the authority of Menu and of the "chief of the saints" (Yajnavalkya), in support of the same doctrine. According to the general consent of the earliest authorities, the filial relation of one of a different class, in default of obtaining one in the same class, is not absolutely denied; but he is regarded merely as prolonging the line, and as entitled to maintenance only from the person succeeding to the estate.

(*a*) Select Reports, vol. VI., 192.

(*b*) Select Reports, vol. III., p. 144.

(*c*) Dattaka Mimansa, s. II., verses 21, 23; Dattaka Chandrika, s. VI., v. 4.

According to Sir Thomas Strange (*a*) such an adoption has, in general, nothing but disqualifying effects:—"parted with by his parents, it divests the child of his natural, without entitling him to the substituted claims incident to an unexceptionable adoption. Incompetent to perform effectually those rites on account of which adoption is resorted to, he cannot inherit to the adopter, but remains a charge upon him entitled only to maintenance."

And even in the *kritrima* form of adoption, this condition is insisted upon and derives additional force from the circumstance that it is the one solitary condition imposed by law in that form of adoption, viz., that the adopter and the adopted should be of the same class.

No case has yet been decided in which the question of the validity of an adoption, in breach of this rule, has been determined. But there can be no reason for carrying the rule beyond the foundation on which it is apparently based, viz., the incapacity of the parents (who assume to contract the adoption) to contract a valid marriage.

The fourth rule (*b*) is in accordance with the doctrine of Vasistha and Saunaka, that *the adoption of a son by any Brahmana must be made from amongst sapindas (the nearer being preferred to the more remote), and only upon failure of these may an adopted son be sought amongst those not so connected.* This rule is, however, merely directory, and not imperative; its neglect does not vitiate the adoption of a remote where a near kinsman exists, or of a stranger where a relative exists.

Sir F. Macnaghten (*c*) lays down the rule in these words: "Brahmins should adopt sons from among their own *sapindas*,

(*a*) Strange's Hindu Law, vol. I., p. 82; and see Sutherland's Synopsis, Head II.

(*b*) Dattaka Mimansa, s. II., v. 2.

(*c*) Considerations of Hindu Law, p. 150.

and on failure of *sapindas*, from among those not *sapindas*. Among *sapindas*, the brother's son is to be considered as the best (*a*). If a brother's son does not exist, a *sapinda*, who is also a *sagotra*, is to be chosen. If such is not to be found, a *sapinda* who is not a *sagotra*. Then comes the *sagotra* who is not a *sapinda*, and lastly one neither a *sagotra* nor a *sapinda*.

The last rule relates to the age of the adopted child. As respects the Kritrima form of adoption, there is no limit and no condition as to the performance of ceremonies. It has even been declared that a man may adopt his own father.

As regards the *dattaka* form, that child is to be preferred whose initiatory rites have not been begun. The final initiatory rite, that of marriage, must be performed in the family of the adopter. Whether tonsure and upanayana in the case of the three higher castes should also be performed in the family of adoption is a point on which there is a difference of opinion between the Dattaka Chandrika and the Dattaka Mimansa, the former being in favour of greater laxity than the latter. The provisions of the former are satisfied if the adoptive father performs those initiatory rites which have yet to be completed, accepting as effective those the natural father has already performed. The author of that treatise (*b*) concludes, as matter of law, that if the rite of investiture merely be performed by the adopter, the previous rites having been performed by the natural father, the filiation of the son given, as son of the adopter, is completed. Thus the investiture with the Brahminical thread in the family of the adopter, under the family name of the adopter, is a sufficient compliance with the rule which requires that regeneration should be effected in the adoptive family.

(*a*) See 9 Menu, 182.

(*b*) Dattaka Chandrika, section II., verses 19, 23.

In the Dattaka Mimansa (*a*), on the other hand, the rule is laid down as propounded in the Kalika Purana, that a son who has once been initiated, as far as the ceremony of tonsure inclusive, under the family name of the natural father, cannot become son to another man. According to the schools which recognise this doctrine, a child so filiated in his natural family cannot be adopted except as a *dwyamushyayana*; and even this effect will only be produced when he is under six years of age at the time of gift, and when his adoptive father repeats the performance of all the initiatory rites down to the ceremony of tonsure, having first annulled the rites already performed by the sacrifice called *putreshti.*

Jagannatha, in his Digest, still further restricts the qualifications or eligibility of the adopted child (*b*); for he insists that if the boy has completed his fifth year, and has thereby passed the proper age for tonsure, he thereby becomes ineligible, unless where the gift and acceptance of the child have taken place before the completion of the fifth year and before tonsure. There has been a comparatively recent decision (*c*) in the Allahabad High Court to the effect that under the Dattaka Mimansa an adoption is valid so long as the boy is below six years of age; and in the judgment an opinion was expressed in favour of the age of the *upanayana* being the material date, and its performance the sole bar to adoption in the case of the three higher castes.

Even as regards the *upanayana* itself being a fatal bar to adoption, Mr. Ellis (*d*), as quoted by Sir T. Strange, says, speaking of an adoption in Southern India:—"With respect to the ineligibility of a person for adoption, on whom the *upanayana* rites have been performed, it is much disputed: the

(*a*) Dattaka Mimansa, section IV., verses 22, *et seq.*

(*b*) Colebrooke's Digest, Book V., Chap. IV., section VIII., verse 273, note.

(*c*) Ganga Sahai *v.* Lekhraj Singh, I. L. R. 9 All., 312.

(*d*) Strange's Hindu Law, vol. II., p. 104.

more correct, *because the more reasonable* opinion would appear to be that he is eligible if of the same *gotra*; ineligible if of a different *gotra* from the adopter; for if of the same *gotra*, the *datta homam,* though proper, is not necessary: if of a different *gotra*, the *datta-homam* is necessary, and it cannot be performed on one who, by the rites of the *upanayana,* has been definitively established in his natural *gotra*." Local usage would readily remove this bar to adoption. And where a child does not pass from one *gotra* to another, there is very little reason in its favour; for adoption within the *gotra* is facilitated and encouraged by the Hindu law-givers.

CHAPTER XVI.

THE EFFECT OF ADOPTION.

The effect of a Kritrima adoption—The rights of inheritance acquired thereby—Effect of dattaka adoption—Rights of adopted son in his natural family—Sapindaship of adopted son in his new gotra—His rights of lineal succession—Of collateral succession—Of succession to cognates—His rights of inheritance *ex parte maternâ*—Loss of heritable right in his natural family—Effect of an invalid adoption.

THE last point to be considered in reference to adoption is the legal effects of the rite or contract upon the *status* and heritable rights of the adopted child. As respects the Kritrima adopted son it has been already pointed out that that mode of adoption does not effect a transfer from one family to another. Accordingly it has been held (*a*) that a son so adopted retains the right of succession and of presenting the funeral cake in his natural family, while he also acquires the same rights in his adoptive family. The son, therefore, of such adopted child can succeed to the estate of his natural father's brother.

The acquired rights of inheritance of a Kritrima son in his adoptive family are strictly limited, the notion of a personal contract between father and son not being lost sight of. He does not become heir to his adoptive father's father, wife, or collateral relation or wife's relations (*b*). He does not transmit any heritable right in the adoptive family to his heirs; the contract being with himself and not with his representatives (*c*).

(*a*) Musst Depeo *v.* Gowreeshunker, Sel Rep., vol. III., p. 307, (new ed.) 410.
(*b*) Shibo Koeree *v.* Joogun Singh, 8 S. W. R., 155.
(*c*) Juswant Singh *v.* Doolee Chund, 25 S. W. R., 255.

It is chiefly necessary to attend to those results which accrue when a valid transfer of a child has been effected from one father to another, or from one *gotra* to another, by a complete *dattaka* adoption. Such a child ceases to have any connection with the natural family, or father, except so far as he is affected by the prohibition to contract marriage therein; and also by the days and seasons of mourning. He is incapable of performing the funeral rites of his natural father, and (*a*) ceases to have any claim upon the family or estate. It is said that the Dattaka son is prohibited from marrying not only within certain degrees in the family of his natural father, but totally in that *gotra*. He is bound to perform the exequial rites to his adopted father, and he is entitled to succeed to his estate, not merely lineally, but also collaterally, in the same way as he would have succeeded had he been a natural son. According to Mr. Sutherland, he also represents the real legitimate son (*b*) in relationship to his adoptive mother; and her ancestry are his maternal grandsires.

Thus the sapindaship of the adopted son is the first question to be disposed of. First, the consanguineal connection involved in that term. Secondly, the connection by the pinda or funeral cake. The sapindaship (*c*) arising from consanguinity cannot be broken; to that extent the relationship of the adopted child to his natural parent's family continues; but with regard to connection by funeral oblations the severance from the natural parents is complete. Upon this subject the text of Vrihat

(*a*) Dattaka Mimansa, section VI., verses 6 and 7.

Menu next propounds another rule:—"A given son must never claim the family and estate of his natural father. The funeral cake follows the family and estate, but of him who has given away his son the obsequies fail."

"The son given must never claim his natural father's family and estate. Thus the obsequies, that is the funeral repast, which would have been performed by the son given, fails of him who has given away his son."

Dattaka Chandrika, section II., verses 18, 19; Sutherland's Synopsis, Head IV.; Vyavastha Darpana, p. 887.

(*b*) Sutherland's Synopsis, Head IV.

(*c*) Vyavastha Darpana, p. 889.

Menu may be quoted: "Sons given, purchased, and the rest retain relations of *sapinda* to the natural father as extending to the fifth and seventh degrees." In the Dattaka Mimansa (*a*) it is explained that the meaning of this passage is, that a consanguineal connection only with the natural family, and not connection by the *pinda,* or funeral cake, remains. On the other hand, no consanguineal tie is formed with the adoptive family; the *sapindaship* which results from adoption is solely a connection by means of the *pinda,* or funeral cake. That connection, it will be seen, extends to only three degrees, while the consanguineal tie extends to seven. When, therefore, we come to enquire what are the prohibitions as to marriage, and the rules as to days of impurity which affect the adopted son in his new family, they will extend only to the third degree (*b*), that being the limit of the relationship formed by adoption. In (*c*) the adoptive family, the rules which regulate the son's oblation of the funeral cake, impurity on occasions of births and deaths, and disability to contract marriage, all stand on the same footing It must, however, be recollected that this can only apply in all its strictness where the adopted son passes from one *gotra* to another. Whatever sanguineal connection there was originally with the adoptive family, will, of course, remain.

It is said by Menu (*d*) that a son of any description must be anxiously adopted by a man destitute of male issue, for the sake of the funeral cake, water, and solemn rites, and for the celebrity of his name. The adopted son, therefore, provided (*e*) he is not displaced by a subsequently born legitimate

(*a*) Dattaka Mimansa, Section VI., verse 10.

(*b*) Dattaka Mimansa, Section VI., verse 32 *et seq.*—When a *dattaka* son passes from one *gotra* to another, there is no reciprocal impurity in the family of the natural father; see Dattaka Chandrika, Section IV., verse 1.

(*c*) Sutherland's Synopsis, Note xx.; Dattaka Mimansa, Section VIII.

(*d*) Dattaka Chandrika, Section I., verse 3.

(*e*) Dattaka Chandrika, Section III., verse 1.

son, performs the adopter's funeral obsequies, the sixteen *shraddhas*, commencing with the first and ending with the *sapindikarana*, the *ekoddista shraddha*, and the *parvana shraddha* (*a*). This latter, however, he does not, like the legitimate son, perform on the anniversary of the day of death. He also presents oblations to the father and other ancestors of his adoptive mother only (*b*), for he is capable of performing the funeral rites of that mother only. This duty is limited to the wife of the adopter (*c*) by whom he was received in adoption; if he were adopted by the husband alone, and not exclusively to any one wife, then he performs the *parvana shraddha* in honour of the ancestors of all such wives.

The right of the adopted son to succeed lineally in the family of his adoptive father is undisputed.

The right to inherit from his collaterals in the same family was first established in 1807 in the case of Shamchunder and Rooderchunder *v.* Narayni Dibeh, in which a double adoption had not been disallowed (*d*). The question submitted to the Pundits was "in the case of two adopted sons of a common adoptive father, can one, on the decease of the other, succeed to his property as his collateral heir?" The answer was in the affirmative, and the Court decreed in accordance with it.

The question of collateral succession in its more general form,—viz., to the estate of the collateral relations of the father, came on for discussion a few years later in the case of Gourhurree Kubraj *v.* Rutnasuree Debia (*e*), where the Pundits, dissenting from the Dayabhaga, concurred with many

(*a*) Vyavastha Darpana, p. 896. And see Post, Chap. XVIII.

(*b*) Dattaka Chandrika, Section III., verse 17.

(*c*) Dattaka Mimansa, Section VI., verse 50.—The forefathers of the adoptive mother only are also the maternal grandsires of sons given, and the rest: for the rule regarding the paternal is equally applicable to the maternal grandsires of adopted sons.

(*d*) Select Reports, Vol. I., p. 209, (new ed.) 279, affirmed 3 Knapp, 55.

(*e*) 6 Sel. Rep., 203.

previous *vyavasthas* which established the adopted son's collateral succession according to the law promulgated by Menu.

And in another case (*a*) the Court held that the daughter of an adopted son could inherit from her father's adoptive collateral relatives. It cited, with approbation, a *vyavastha* of the Pundits (*b*) to the effect "that a valid adopted son must be considered as a member of the *gotra* of his adopting father, and legally entitled to the property of his adopting father's *sapindas*."

But in ruling that an adopted son succeeds collaterally as well as lineally in the family of his adoptive father, it stated that the ruling was limited to succession to the property of *sapindas*, agnates to the adoptive father; with respect to *bandhus* or cognate relations, the ruling had no concern, the question not arising before them. This was the third case in which the Sudder Court, administering the Hindu law of Bengal, had disregarded the authority of the Dayabhaga on this point. In later cases (*c*) it has been held that, beyond all doubt, an adopted son succeeds collaterally, as well as lineally, to the inheritance within the family of his adoptive father. And as regards cognates in the adoptive family, the right of the adopted son to succeed to them has not many years ago been decided in his favour by the Privy Council (*d*).

Next as to his rights of inheritance *ex parte maternâ*. According to Mr. Sutherland (*e*) he represents the real legitimate son not merely in his relationship to his

(*a*) Lokenath Roy *v.* Shamasoondery, S. D. Dec. (1858), p. 1863.

(*b*) Select Reports, Vol. VI., p. 203.

(*c*) Sumbho Chunder Chowdhry *v.* Naraini Debia, 5 S. W. R. P.C., p. 100. Guru Gobind *v.* Anand Lal, 5 B. L. R., 15.

(*d*) Pudma Coomari Debi *v.* The Court of Wards, L. R. 8 Ind. App., 229.

(*e*) Suth. Syn. Head four.

adoptive father and his paternal ancestors, but also in relationship to his adoptive mother and her paternal ancestors. Such rule is founded on the authority both of the Dattaka Mimansa (*a*) and of the Dattaka Chandrika (*b*). The former lays it down that the forefathers of the adoptive mother only are also the maternal ancestors of sons given; but that an adopted son forms no relationship to his adoptive mother's maternal ancestors. The latter authority also lays it down that the *dattaka* adopted son presents oblations to the father and the other paternal ancestors of his adoptive mother only, for he is only capable of performing the funeral rites of that mother. Both authors, therefore, exclude all relationship of such child to the adoptive mother's co-wife and her ancestors.

It may here be remarked that, as a man's right to adopt is as respects his wives absolute, it follows that, if he adopts generally, that is, to himself, both or all his wives become, by virtue of that act, adoptive mothers. But there is no text or primitive rule of law which prevents a husband from joining one wife, to the exclusion of any other wife he may have with him in the act of adoption. Nor is there any rule which expressly permits it. So far as such a rule is recognised, it follows that that wife only who joins in the adoption becomes an adoptive mother (*c*). And further, with regard to a permission to adopt, it follows that that widow alone who has authority from her husband can become an adoptive mother; the co-widows have no relationship to the adopted child.

The adopted son's right of inheritance, *ex parte maternâ*, was in the case of Teencourie Chatterjee *v.* Dinonath Banerjee (*d*) limited to the mother's stridhana, and stated not to include her estate derived from her paternal ancestors; and a Full Bench

(*a*) Section VI., v. 50. (*b*) Dattaka Chandrika, Section III., v. 17.

(*c*) See Kasheshuree *v.* Greeschunder Lahoree, S. W. R. (1864), 71.

(*d*) 3 S. W. R., 49.

in Bengal decided that he cannot succeed to the estate of his adoptive maternal grandfather in priority to male collaterals (*a*); although it had been previously decided that the relations of an adoptive mother inherit the property of her adopted son, just as they would inherit the property of her natural son (*b*). But the Allahabad High Court practically decided that an adopted son had all the rights of a natural born son, and would succeed in the maternal line, taking the estate which descended from his mother's father (*c*). A Calcutta case adopted that view and the Privy Council in appeal affirmed it (*d*); and in Bengal it has since been held that the adopted son of one daughter and the natural son of another daughter shared equally the estate of the maternal grandfather (*e*).

It is, however, quite clear that an adopted son loses all claim upon the family and estates of his natural parents. He has no title to succeed therein, either lineally or collaterally. Nor have the members of the family, which he has quitted, any title to succeed to the estate left by him or his heirs. They are entire strangers to his estate, ancestral or self-acquired. In Madras, an attempt was unsuccessfully made by the natural relations of an adopted child to make out a title by inheritance to his property (*f*). It was held that all rights of inheritance between him and them had been extinguished by the complete severance which had taken place.

Where a son is born, after the parents have received a child in adoption, according to some copies of the texts of Katyayana, and according to the authority of Vasishta (*g*), such adopted

(*a*) Morun Moyee Debia *v.* Bejoy Kishan Gossamer, Suth. F. B. R., p. 121.

(*b*) S. D. A. (1859), p. 1091.

(*c*) Sham Kuar *v.* Gaya, I. L. R. 1 All., 256.

(*d*) Kali Komul *v.* Uma Shunkur, L. R. 10 I. A., 138.

(*e*) Surjokant Nundi *v.* Moheschunder, I. L. R. 9 Cal., 70.

(*f*) See Srinivasa Ayyangar *v.* Kuppan Ayyangar, Mad. H. C. R., Vol. I., p. 180.

(*g*) Dattaka Chandrika, s. V., verses 16, 17.

son takes a fourth share of the ancestral estate. The rule of law, so laid down, is accepted by the schools other than that of Bengal. They apparently follow the author of the Mitakshara (*a*). The Bengal school, on the other hand, follows the teaching of Jimutavahana (*b*), who, on the authority of a text of Devala, and other copies of the text of Katyayana, prescribes one-third.

With regard to the succession of sons who are adopted by disqualified persons, assuming such adoption to be valid, as it is nowhere authoritatively prohibited, such sons have no right to succeed to the estate of the adoptive grandfather; maintenance alone can be claimed by them according to the authority of the Dattaka Chandrika (*c*).

Maintenance also is frequently assigned where the ceremony of adoption is by any reason invalid for the purpose of creating affiliation, but nevertheless sufficient to effect the separation of a child from his natural parents. The Madras High Court assumed the existence of such a rule to be correct in a case (*d*) decided in 1862, but the next year the same Court held that there was nothing in Hindu law which would warrant a claim to maintenance, where there was no valid adoption (*e*) notwithstanding the authorities which they referred to, which were Mr. Strange's Manual, ss. 120 and 197; Strange's Hindu Law, Vol. I., p. 82; Dattaka Chandrika, s. I., clauses 14, 15, and s. 6, clause 4. The case was one, however, in which it was claimed that an invalidly adopted son could transmit to his son and heir a right to be maintained out of the estate of his alleged adoptive father.

(*a*) Mitakshara, Chap. I., s. XI., v. 24.

(*b*) Dayabhaga, Chap. X., v. 7.

(*c*) Dattaka Chandrika, s. VI., v. 1.

(*d*) Ayyavu Muspanar *v.* Niladatchi Ammal, Mad. H. C. R., Vol. I., p. 45.

(*e*) Bawani Sankara Pandit *v.* Ambabay Ammal, Mad. H. C. R., Vol. I., p. 363.

It appears also that a widow (*a*) who exercises a power to adopt, after her husband's estate has vested elsewhere than in herself, cannot confer on her child any rights of inheritance, but only, if anything, a title to be maintained out of the estate, or at least by herself. The case in which such adopted son was held to be without any title to succeed to the estates of his adoptive mother's husband is an extremely important one, as it shows conclusively that it is only the last full independent owner whose permission to adopt will be valid to all purposes including those of inheritance. If a Hindu neglects to adopt, the widow of his father may repair the omission so far as the obsequies of her husband and his ancestors are concerned; but it is not in her power to render the ancestral estate answerable for those charges, or to affect its devolution in any way, except in the case where her husband's estate has eventually vested in her as heiress to her son or other successor to her husband.

(*a*) Mussamut Bhoobun Moyee Debia *v.* Ram Kishore Acharj Chowdhry, 10 Moore, I. A., p. 304; s. c., 3 W. R. P.C., p. 15.

CHAPTER XVII.

THE LAW OF SUCCESSION.

Succession by survivorship—Modified by the doctrine of representation—Rights by survivorship paramount to those of creditors of the deceased—Depends on status of the family and the nature of the property—Effect of survivorship on the rights of the widow and of creditors—The Shivagunga case—Two courses of descent in the same family—Succession to impartible estate.

SUCCESSION under Hindu law is by survivorship or by inheritance. Succession by survivorship is the rule with regard to joint families under the Mitakshara, where the property belongs to the family, the members of which are constantly changing as successive births and deaths occur. Succession by inheritance is the rule in reference to all property which is held in severalty by an absolute title, whether it was self acquired, or, as in Bengal, held jointly with others, but by a separate title as regards each separate and defined share; or, as under the Mitakshara, by the last surviving coparcener.

The earliest form, therefore, of succession is by survivorship; the only remaining traces of which are to be found in the law of the Mitakshara. By that law the property of the family vests in all its male members to the third degree, with the occasional exception of some one of them, who may be under a legal disability to hold or exercise proprietary rights. The parcenership of each member commences with his birth, his rights, however, dating back to the moment of conception. In the same way it terminates with death, or with any other event which in law prevents a man from being the owner of property. And thereupon the surviving male members of the family become the owners of its estate by the strictest application of the doctrine of survivorship; their relations to one another in respect of the share to which each will be entitled on partition being modified by applying the doctrine of individual representation.

In this way it cannot be said that the law of inheritance has no application to joint families under the Mitakshara. Though the immediate result is that all the existing male members continue to be the joint owners, yet their relative rights *inter se*, that is, the shares to which they will be severally entitled on a partition being effected, are modified by the law of inheritance. So long as they are all sons of the same father they will be entitled on partition to equal shares; as each son dies his sons will be entitled to divide his share equally between them; in case he leaves no male issue his surviving brothers, but not their descendants whilst one brother survives, will divide his share to the exclusion of his widow, who will be entitled to maintenance only. Strictly speaking, therefore, the succession by survivorship lasts only till partition is effected. The rights of the members of the family at partition, and also with a view to partition, are determined by the law of inheritance, except so far as, in particular cases, succession by survivorship has excluded succession by inheritance.

The extent to which it does so is for all practical purposes very limited; though it constitutes the chief point of difference between the Bengal and Mitakshara schools. The right by survivorship is sufficient to exclude the right of any creditor of the deceased, and in some parts of India even of his purchaser to follow the share of his debtor, unless he has obtained a charge thereon by legal process. The right by survivorship is paramount to such claims while the right by inheritance would be subject to them. The extent to which succession by survivorship still excludes succession by inheritance or representation is explained in a judgment of the High Court of Bengal in the Full Bench decision of the case of Sadabart Prasad Sahu *v.* Foolbash Koer (*a*): "According to the Mitakshara law, if a member of a joint undivided family dies without a son, and leaving a brother, his widow does not take his share by descent. If he leaves a son, the son takes by descent; but if he leaves only a widow the survivors take by survivorship, and they hold the property which they take by survivorship legally and equitably for themselves, and not in trust for the heirs of the deceased. The heirs of the deceased have no interest either legally or equitably in the share which passes by survivorship to the surviving co-sharer. That will be made very clear if you suppose the case of a joint family consisting of a father and two sons and two uncles, the brothers of the father, taking property by descent from the father of the father and of the two uncles. The father and the two sons take one-third, and the two uncles each take one-third—that is, they take that which, upon partition, would be allotted. Then suppose that one of the sons dies without issue, leaving a widow, such widow, according to the Mitakshara law, would not take his share in the estate. Then the question is, would it go to the person who would be heir if the widow was dead or had not existed? It clearly does not go to the heir, because the heir would be the surviving brother and not the father. If it would go to the heir, the surviving brother would take the whole of the interest of the deceased brother, but the law is that it goes by survivorship, and the survivors take legally and equitably for themselves, and not in trust for the brother of the deceased. Neither the widow of the deceased nor his brother would take any interest by inheritance from the deceased in the joint family estate."

Accordingly succession by survivorship, where it really takes effect in regulating the rights of individuals, depends upon two

(*a*) 3 B. L. R. (F. B.), p. 34.

circumstances—viz., the *status* of the family, and the nature of the proprietary interest which belonged to the deceased. If the family were joint and the estate were held under Mitakshara law by coparceners as joint estate, and a coparcener died without male issue, the succession will be by survivorship pure and simple. If the deceased coparcener left male issue, the law of inheritance will determine what shares such issue will be entitled to upon partition. If he left self-acquired estate the law of inheritance and not survivorship will apply to it at the moment of death.

It is the right of the widow of the deceased, or of his creditors, which is chiefly affected by the question whether his property passes by survivorship or by inheritance. Under Mitakshara law the widow has no interest in such of her husband's property as passes by survivorship. When he dies without male issue and separated from his brethren, then her title to succeed is by inheritance and is prior to that of separated collateral heirs.

The widow's right is discussed in the second chapter of the Mitakshara, which declares the correct law to be that (*a*) "when a man who was separated from his co-heirs and not reunited with them dies, leaving no male issue, his widow, if chaste, takes the estate, in the first instance."

On the other hand, the author of the Dayabhaga (c. XI.), discussing the same texts as the Mitakshara and others to the same effect, rejects the notion of a right by survivorship altogether, and also the doctrine which limits the widow's right of succession to the estates of her separated husband.

The Shivagunga case (*b*) is the leading authority upon the position of a Hindu widow under the Mitakshara. The Privy Council held that her right was governed by the nature of the property and not by the *status* of the husband; in other words

(*a*) Mitakshara, Chap. II., s. 1, v. 30.

(*b*) Kattama Nauchear *v.* Rajah of Shivagunga, 2 S. W. R. P.C., 31.

it depended not upon whether he was joint in other respects with his brethren, but upon whether the estate which his sonless widow claimed to inherit had been held by him separately or in coparcenary.

Consequently two courses of descent may exist to the same person. His estate held in coparcenary will, on failure of male issue, pass by survivorship to his coparceners; his estate self-acquired, or otherwise held in severalty, will on failure of male issue pass by inheritance to his widow. This rule is an old one, but after some conflict of opinion it was finally established by the Privy Council. They said that two courses of descent may obtain on a part division of joint property; relying on a passage in Macnaghten's Hindu Law (*a*) in these words: 'According to the more correct opinion, where there is an undivided residue, it is not subject to the ordinary rules of partition of joint property. In other words, if, at a general partition, any part of the property was left joint, the widow of a deceased brother will not participate, notwithstanding the separation, but such undivided residue will go exclusively to the brother.' They proceeded:—

"Again, it is not pretended that, on the death of the acquirer of separate property, the separately acquired property falls into the common stock, and passes like ancestral property. On the contrary, it is admitted that, if the acquirer leaves male issue, it will descend as separate property to that issue down to the third generation. Although, therefore, when there is male issue, the family property and the separate property would not descend to different persons—they would descend in a different way, and with different consequences, the sons taking their father's share in the ancestral property, subject to all the rights of the coparceners in that property, and his self-acquired property, free from those rights. The course of succession would

(*a*) Page 53.

not be the same for the family estate and the separate estate; and it is clear, therefore, that, according to the Hindu law, there need not be unity of heirship.

"But to look more closely into the Hindu law. When property belonging in common to a united Hindu family has been divided, the divided shares go in the general course of descent of separate property. Why, it may well be asked, should not the same rule apply to property which, from its first acquisition, has always been separate? We have seen from the passage already quoted from Macnaghten's Hindu Law that, when a residue is left undivided upon partition, what is divided goes as separate property, what is undivided follows the family property—that which remains as it was, devolves in the old line; that which is changed and becomes separate, devolves in the new line. In other words, the law of succession follows the nature of the property and the interest in it."

It follows then from this, that the right by survivorship depends both upon the *status* of the family and also the nature of the estate. It obtains only in joint families under Mitakshara law, and in regard to joint estate. If an estate has been self-acquired by one, the other members of the joint family have no interest in it and cannot claim by survivorship. An impartible estate, however, may be joint as well as separate (*a*). It is not the separate enjoyment but the separate title to which the law looks in deciding between the rival claim of the widow and the surviving coparceners. This discussion clearly brings out the slight degree in which the principle of succession by survivorship, the normal principle amongst communities like the Hindu joint family, still retains any influence over the devolution of property. It is treated by the Privy Council as one which merely tends to qualify the rule which gives the

(*a*) Stree Rajah Yanumula Venkayamah *v.* Stree Rajah Yanumula Boochi Venkondora, see 13 Sutherland's Weekly Reporter, P.C., p. 21; and see also 3 B. L. R. P.C., 41.

inheritance to widows; its operation is merely an exception to that of the ordinary law of Hindu inheritance, which in the time of Jimutavahana, was exclusively based upon religious doctrine, without any exception in favour of survivorship, regardless of the ordinary usage of the communal system.

Succession by survivorship applies only to Mitakshara joint families while they continue joint; and in its practical consequences interposes the rights of the survivors between the deceased member and those who would have had either by inheritance or contract claims against his estate if it had been separate.

CHAPTER XVIII.

THE LAW OF INHERITANCE.

Law of the shraddha—Differences between the Dayabhaga and the Mitakshara on inheritance—Sapindaship under the two schools—Connection through the pinda explained—Limits of the sapinda connection—Its collateral branches—Sapindaship of women—Bandhus—Saculyas—Samanodakas—Nature of the shraddha—Brief account of the ceremonies—Parvana shraddha—Sapindikarana.

THE law of the shraddha is said to be the key of the whole Hindu law of inheritance. Yet it is stated, upon high authority (*a*), that there is scarcely a trace in the unwritten customs of Hindus of the existence of the doctrine which now prevails—viz., that of spiritual benefit to the deceased determining the order of succession to his estate. However that may be, it is a doctrine which is common to all the existing schools of Hindu law, and is the basis upon which the law of the Dayabhaga, the latest development of that law, exclusively rests. And it may easily be conjectured that an early innovation upon the archaic type of the family with its rights of survivorship, one of the first results of individual energy beginning to break loose from the trammels of the corporate system, was the introduction of a rule, by which the lineal male descendants succeeded to

(*a*) Maine's Village Communities, p. 53. "I have been assured from many quarters that one sweeping theory, which dominates the whole codified law, can barely be traced in the unwritten customs. It sounds like a jest to say that, according to the principles of Hindu law, property is regarded as the means of paying a man's funeral expenses, but this is not so very untrue of the written law concerning which the most dignified of the Indian Courts has recently laid down, after an elaborate examination of all the authorities, that the right of inheritance, according to Hindu law, is wholly regulated with reference to the spiritual benefits to be conferred on the deceased proprietor."

the place or interest of a deceased member of a joint family by a title paramount to the general right by survivorship.

It must be recollected that the rules which regulate the devolution of property by inheritance amongst Hindus are, at the present day, based upon the same principle in all the schools—viz., that of spiritual benefit. The chief points of difference between them, to which it is important to pay attention in order to understand the general scope and spirit of the existing Hindu law of inheritance, are the following:

First of all, there is the retention of a right of the older form of succession by survivorship in the Mitakshara joint family, the nature and extent of which has been explained.

Secondly, the preference of particular schools for certain special texts, to meet the case of particular persons.

Thirdly, there is some recognition of the claims of blood relationship by the older school, in which the term "sapinda" denotes consanguinity as well as connexion by funeral oblations. But in the Bengal school, at least for purposes of inheritance, the relationship denoted by the word "sapinda" is exclusively that of connexion by the funeral cake—*i.e.*, the relationship between those who give, receive, and participate in the same funeral offerings.

Fourthly, the more general exclusion of females by the later school from the order of succession, and the refusal to them of absolute proprietary interest. In the older form of the law, although females were as a body postponed to the males of a family, still they, in their turn, took in preference to the members of a different family; and it would appear that they took a larger proprietary right than is now accorded to them. The order of succession became more favourable to the heritable classes of males, as the doctrine of spiritual benefit prevailed.

Fifthly, the mode in which the successive classes of heirs are arranged. Under the Mitakshara the cognates as a body, that is those relations who are members of a different family from the deceased, are postponed to the gentiles or those of the same family. In the Dayabhaga, the classes of heirs are *Sapindas, Sakulyas* and *Samanodakas.* In each class there are members of a different family or families from that of the deceased. That circumstance, however, though it affects the internal arrangement of each class, does not in any other way determine the order of priority. A *Sapinda* sprung of a different family will take precedence of a *Sakulya* sprung of the same family.

These are the chief points in which the existing schools differ from each other. The author of the Dayabhaga is the most determined as well as the latest exponent of the principle upon which the law of succession and inheritance is avowedly, and in the Bengal school exclusively, based. And, accordingly, in treating of that law in detail, it is convenient to do so by the light of his treatise, pointing out from time to time the variations between his doctrines, which belong to the most advanced school of Hindu law, and those of other schools which still retain some of the older usages.

To understand the principles and order of succession by inheritance according to the Dayabhaga it is necessary to understand the relationship which is constituted by connection through the *pinda* or funeral cake.

The definition of *sapinda* may be taken from Mr. Justice Dwarkanath Mitter in his judgment delivered in the case of Amrita Kumari Debi *v.* Lakhinarayan Chuckerbutty (*a*), in which the position of sister's son, as a *bandhu*, and therefore as an heir, was declared. He says: "It is a well-known principle of Hindu law, recognised in all the schools current in the country, that the relation of *sapinda* exists not only between the immediate giver and the immediate recipient

(*a*) 2 Bengal Law Reports, F. B., p. 33.

of funeral oblations, but also between those who are bound to offer them to a common ancestor or ancestors. This principle is based upon the theory according to which a Hindu is supposed to participate after his death in the funeral oblations that are offered by any one of his surviving relations to some common ancestor, to whom he himself was bound to offer them while living; and hence it is that the man who gives the oblations and the man who receives them, and the man who participates in them, are all recognised as *sapindas* of each other. Thus, for example, brothers are not required to perform the obsequies of each other, but they are nevertheless *sapindas*, being connected with each other through the medium of the oblation which they are respectively bound to offer to their common ancestors. The same rule holds good in the case of the brother's son, and in fact of every *sapinda* who does not stand in a direct line of ascent or descent with the deceased proprietor himself."

Connection through the *pinda*, therefore, denotes relationship through giving, receiving or participating in funeral oblations offered to a deceased ancestor. From the earliest period of Hindu history the obligation to present funeral offerings extended to the ancestor in three degrees (*a*). "To three," says Menu, "must libations of water be made, to three must oblations of food be presented; the fourth in descent is the giver of those offerings, but the fifth has no concern with them." A Hindu, therefore, is bound to offer funeral oblations to his father, grandfather, and great-grandfather; and also in right of his mother, and in the fulfilment of duties of *sapindaship* which she is disqualified from discharging, but which she owes to her ancestors, he must also offer funeral oblations to her father, grandfather, and great-grandfather in the male line.

(*a*) Menu, IX. 186, as cited in Dayabhaga, Chap. XI., s. 6, v. 7.

In his turn he is entitled to receive those oblations from his son, his grandson, and his great-grandson in the male line, and also from his daughter's son, who offers them in right of his mother.

So far with regard to the direct line, the limits of the relationship include seven degrees, three in ascent and three in descent from the living proprietor in the male line. It differs from the agnatic relationship in at least two important particulars, namely, that there is a limit imposed both in the scale of ascent and descent beyond which you cannot trace this connection; and, secondly, the principle of *mulier est finis familiæ* is not observed, but the woman's duties of *sapindaship* devolve upon her son, and he is for those purposes included in his maternal family. But her sons are her only descendants who derive from her the connection through the *pinda* with her family; her daughters and her son's sons and daughters are all excluded.

Then as respects collateral branches, connection by the *pinda* depends upon the same principle, and we have to ascertain who amongst them are bound to offer oblations to the same ancestor. For example, the proprietor's brothers and their sons and grandsons all offer oblation to the father of the proprietor, and, therefore, they are included amongst his *sapindas*. His paternal uncles, again, and their sons and grandsons offer to his grandfather and great-grandfather; so also the brothers of his grandfather and their sons and grandsons offer to his great-grandfather. There is a limit therefore, in all directions, lineally and collaterally, to the connection between kindred by means of the funeral cake. The nearness or remoteness of that connection is measured by the nearness or remoteness of the common ancestor whose obsequies such kindred are bound to perform.

The place which women occupy in reference to *sapindaship* is, perhaps, somewhat singular. They are the *sapindas* of all with whom their brothers are *sapindas*. But their duties devolve upon their sons, who stand in their place, and are bound to offer funeral cakes to their fathers, grandfathers, and great-grandfathers. Such sons, in consequence, include as their *sapindas* all with whom their mother's brothers are *sapindas*, but they do not transmit to their descendants the duties or the connection, which terminate with them.

Sapindas thus connected through a female are an exception to the otherwise exclusively agnatic character of the *sapinda* relationship. They are called *bandhus*, *i.e.*, kinsmen sprung from a different family but allied by funeral oblations (*a*). These, according to the Mitakshara, are of three kinds, *i.e.*, *bandhus* to the person himself, to his father, or to his mother. Such enumeration, if exhaustive, would restrict the *sapinda* relationship through a female within very narrow limits. The Privy Council, in the case of Gridhari Lal Roy *v.* Government of Bengal (*b*), treated this restriction as arbitrary and inconsistent with the definition as given in the Mitakshara. They ruled that a maternal uncle was *bandhu* to the deceased, and the Full Bench of the High Court, by the judgment of Mr. Justice Mitter above referred to, ruled that the sister's son was *bandhu* to the deceased *Bandhus*, therefore, by the Mitakshara, as well as by the law of Bengal (*c*), where no doubt on the subject ever existed, include all *sapindas* whose relationship to one another is traced through a female. They are necessarily a limited class, for the *pinda* relationship through a female terminates with her son.

The lineal relations beyond the fourth degree in ascent or descent, *i.e.*, above the great-grandfather of the living proprietor, and also below his great-grandson, are not included in the list of

(*a*) Mitakshara, Chap. II., s. 6.

(*b*) 1 Bengal Law Reports, P.C., p. 51.

(*c*) See the Dayabhaga, Chap. XI., s. 6, vv. 13, 14.

his *sapindas.* But the great-grandfather was himself, when alive, the centre of a circle of *sapindas* which upwards included three generations of such ancestors, and extended downwards to include the living proprietor. Those three male ancestors in the degrees above the great-grandfather are not, however, *sapindas* of the living proprietor, but stand towards him in a relationship denominated *saculyas.* They and he are *sapindas* to the same person in a line of ascent or descent, *i.e.*, are the *sapindas* of the great-grandfather, and are therefore *saculyas* of each other. *Saculyas*, or distant kinsmen (*a*), are those who share the divided oblation, *i.e.*, who share the remains of the oblation wiped off with *kusá* grass. They include, therefore, the three generations above and below those previously described as the *sapindas* of the living proprietor. They are ascertained upon the same principles as are applied to determine *sapindas*, extending the connection so that the living proprietor is seventh instead of fourth in ascent or descent. Such *saculyas* are also termed his *sapindas* for some purposes.

Last in order come the class of *samanodakas*, or kindred connected by a common libation of water, and they must be understood to reach to seven degrees beyond the kindred connected by funeral oblation of food; or else, as far as the limits of knowledge as to birth and name extend. According to the text of the Mitakshara, "if there be none such" (alluding to kindred of the same family connected by funeral oblations) "the succession devolves on kindred connected by libations of water; and they must be understood to reach to seven degrees beyond the kindred connected by funeral oblations of food; or

(*a*) Colebrooke's Digest, B.V., Chap. VIII., s. 1, v. 435. "The fourth person and the rest share the remains of the oblation wiped off with *kusá* grass; the father and the rest share the funeral cakes; the seventh person is the giver of oblations; the relation of *sapindas*, or men connected by the funeral cake, extends therefore to the seventh person, or sixth degree of ascent or descent."

(*b*) See Mitakshara, Chap. II., s. 5, v. 6.

else, as far as the limits of knowledge as to birth and name extend. Accordingly, Vrihat Menu says, the relation of the *sapindas,* or kindred connected by the funeral oblation, ceases with the seventh person; and that of *samanodakas,* or those connected by a common libation of water, extends to the fourteenth degree, or, as some affirm, it reaches as far as the meaning of birth and name extends, this is signified by *gotra* or the relation of family name."

A word must be added as to the nature of the shraddha, or funeral obsequies, which form, as it were, the link which binds seven successive generations together, which determine the pinda relationship, which underlie the law of inheritance. These obsequies consist of oblations of food and libations of water, which it is the duty of a Hindu to offer to the manes of his ancestors, without which they will be tormented with hunger and thirst, and repulsed from a region of bliss, while the sonless man will sink into *put,* or the region of everlasting torment. The presence of a son, natural or adopted, to perform the ceremony is indispensable to its complete spiritual efficacy, and occasions the anxiety which pervades the community for the possession of male offspring. In the Dattaka Mimansa it is said that a Brahmana, immediately on being born, is produced a debtor in three obligations: to the holy saints, for the practice of religious duties; to the gods, for the performance of sacrifice; to his forefathers, for offspring. "By a son," says Menu, "a man obtains victory over all people; by a son's son, he enjoys immortality; and afterwards by the son of that grandson he reaches the solar abode" (*a*). The reason is added that without him the obsequies would fail (*b*); the most significant rites of

(*a*) 9 Menu, p. 137.

(*b*) See Colebrooke's Digest, B. V., Chap. IX., s. 2, sl. 514. "The first rites must be performed; but the last rites shall only be celebrated by sons and the rest." And in a note it is added "The first funeral ceremony is the cremation of the corpse; the middle rites consist in gathering the ashes and performing the obsequies for a person recently deceased—these extend to the first annual *shraddha;* the last rites are the monthly, annual, and other obsequies for ancestors long since deceased."

the *shraddha* (*a*), *i.e.*, the *parvana shraddha*, performed by those who succeed in the direct line, would fail; and unaided by the *puttra* (son), the soul of the Hindu must sink into that *put* from which it is the province of the son to deliver him (*a*).

The following account of the ceremony is derived from a paper contributed to the 7th volume of the Asiatic Researches, by Mr. Colebrooke (*b*). It commences with the preparation by the sons of a funeral pile, on a spot which is duly consecrated. Then follows the cremation, or burning, which is so managed that some of the bones remain for the subsequent ceremony of burning the ashes. Libations of water are offered to the deceased after the burning. Ten days of mourning (*c*) ensue, and then his son, or nearest kinsman, gathers his ashes and offers a *shraddha,* singly, for him. Food is then distributed to the assembled *Brahmanas.* Then spreading *kusá* grass near the fragments of the repast, he distributes rice and sprinkles water thereon with suitable prayers, naming the deceased, and saying "may this oblation be acceptable to thee." He afterwards takes a cake or ball (*pinda*) of food, and presents it saying, "may this cake be acceptable to thee;" and again sprinkles water on the ground to wash the oblations; the priests offering salutations to the gods, and repeating texts.

In these, the first funeral obsequies, the object in view is to effect, by means of oblations, the re-embodying the soul of the deceased, after burning his corpse. The houses and persons of the mourners must then be purified; and after that, the second obsequies begin, the object of which is to raise the shade of the

(*a*) Shamachurn's Vyavastha Darpana, p. 740. The substitute for a son is necessary, notwithstanding a widow's capacity to present the oblations of food and libations of water to the manes of her husband; for the son is required chiefly to perform the *parvana shraddha* to deliver the father from the hell called "*put,*" and to prolong his lineage, which are beyond the capacity of a widow.

(*b*) Vol. VII., pp. 232-262.

(*c*) That is in the case of Brahmins, twelve in the case of Kshatryas, fifteen in the case of Vaisyas, and one month in the case of Sudras.

L

deceased from this world (where else it would continue to roam amongst demons and evil spirits) up to heaven, and there beatify him, as it were, amongst the manes of his departed ancestors.

These ceremonies, in honour of a single ancestor, are denominated the *ekodishta shraddha.* They are offered, according to a note to Colebrooke's Digest, monthly, during the first year; two extra *shraddhas* being performed before the end of the 6th and 12th month respectively, making, with the ceremony of cremation and the final ceremony, sixteen *shraddhas* in all (*a*).

The *shraddha* in honour of progenitors is termed *parvana shraddha.* It is the offering of a double set of oblations at the *parva,* viz., three cakes to the father, paternal grandfather, and great-grandfather, and three to the maternal grandfather, his father and grandfather, and the remnants to each set of the three remoter ancestors of each line (*b*). It is in abeyance, and cannot be performed, after the death of their next male descendant, until the *sapindikarana* in his honour have been performed.

The *sapindikarana* is the rite of associating the deceased with the manes of the departed ancestors by admixture of the *pindas* before described, and in strictness it should take place on the anniversary of the day of the death (*c*), and combines

(*a*) See Colebrooke's Digest, B. V., C. VIII., section 1, sl. 399. "Sixteen *shraddhas* must be performed for a *Brahmana* recently deceased. The first on the day immediately following the period of mourning; twelve monthly oblations; one additional *shraddha* before the expiration of the sixth month; another before the expiration of the year; and lastly the *sapindikarana,* or first annual obsequies, performed on the anniversary of his death. Thenceforward, obsequies should be annually celebrated for an ancestor on the date of his death, besides monthly *shraddhas* and other ceremonies directed by Menu in the third chapter of his Institutes (See 3 Menu, 247). In Mithila and some other provinces, the obsequies for a *Brahmana* recently deceased are abridged, and by a fiction completed on the second day after mourning."

(*b*) Shamachurn's Vyavastha Darpana, p. 20.

(*c*) Shamachurn's Vyavastha Darpana, p. 898. *Sapindikarana* is the rite of associating the deceased with the manes of the departed ancestors by admixture of *pindas* (oblation balls or cakes of rice, &c.). It should strictly take place on the anniversary of the day of death; but in the case of the deceased leaving an only son, or no son, it may also be performed at any time within one year from the deceased's death after the performance of the fourteen monthly *shraddhas* called *masikas.*

the last *ekodishta shraddha,* or obsequies performed singly for the deceased, with the *parvana shraddha,* or obsequies which the deceased was in the habit of offering in his lifetime to his three immediate ancestors in the male line—his father, grandfather, and great-grandfather. Thenceforth the deceased is associated with his three ancestors, and the last obsequies have been paid to the great-grandfather; and the next *parvana shraddha* will be in honour of the deceased, his father, and grandfather. Previous to the performance of the *sapindikarana* the deceased is not denominated a "pitri" or departed ancestor (*a*).

(*a*) For a description of it see Dattaka Mimansa, s. 6, note.

CHAPTER XIX.

ON LINEAL INHERITANCE.

Order of succession based on spiritual benefit to the deceased—Lineal male succession—Per stirpes—Illegitimate sons—Extent of their rights—The widow—Several widows—Condition as to chastity—Rights of widow after re-marriage—Daughter—Precedence amongst daughters under the Mitakshara and Bengal schools—Extent of the daughter's right—In Bombay—Daughters' sons—Bandhus in lineal descent—Mother—Stepmother—Father—Grandparents.

THE doctrine of the Dayabhaga and of the treatises founded upon it, whose authority is current in Bengal, is that by considerations of spiritual benefit alone the whole order of succession is to be determined. Menu (*a*), it points out (*b*), had emphatically declared :—" To the nearest sapinda the inheritance next belongs." That the sapindaship here meant is not consanguinity but the tie of the *pinda*, which connects three generations in ascent and three in the descending scale with the living proprietor, is shown by the direction contained in the preceding verse of Menu, who specifies the fourth in descent as the giver of those oblations, and distinctly excludes the fifth in descent from being heir, because he is not connected by a single oblation; excludes him, that is, so long as a person connected by a single oblation, whether sprung from the father's or the mother's family, exists. The Dayabhaga denies in express terms that Menu's text—" to the nearest sapinda the inheritance next belongs "—was ever intended to indicate nearness of kin

(*a*) 9 Menu, v. 187.

(*b*) Dayabhaga, Chap. XI., s. 6, v. 17.

according to the order of birth (*a*) It concludes that the order of succession must be obtained by discriminating kinsmen according to the degrees of their proximity in their alliance by common oblations (*b*). For it is reasonable, he adds, that the wealth which a man has acquired should be made beneficial to him by appropriating it according to the degree in which services are rendered to him.

A Full Bench judgment (*c*) of the High Court of Bengal, delivered by Mr. Justice Dwarkanath Mitter, establishes this doctrine as the basis of the order of succession. "It is beyond all dispute," he says, "that the whole of that portion of the Dayabhaga which is devoted to the subject is nothing but a mere elaboration of the doctrine of spiritual benefit. Every point for which a discussion is thought necessary is ultimately determined by that doctrine; and it is by that doctrine that every difficulty is ultimately removed. The texts of Menu and various other Hindu sages are frequently cited, it is true, as the highest authorities on Hindu law; but it is by the light of the doctrine of spiritual benefit that every one of those texts is interpreted, and it is by that light that every discrepancy existing between them is reconciled."

The first rule which results from this principle is in the language of Menu (*d*) :—"Not brothers, nor parents, but sons if living, or their male issue, are heirs to the deceased; but of him who leaves no son, nor a wife, nor a daughter, the father shall take the inheritance; and if he leave neither father nor mother, the brothers." The inheritance therefore descends lineally, in the first instance, to sons, grandsons, and great-grandsons. If more than one son, they take in equal shares;

(*a*) Dayabhaga, Chap. XI., s. 6, v. 18.

(*b*) Ibid., v. 19.

(*c*) Guru Gobind Shaha Mundul *v.* Anand Lal Ghose Mozoomdar, 5 B. L. R., 36.

(*d*) 9 Menu, v. 185.

but if a son has pre-deceased his father, his share is taken by the grandson or great-grandson, as the case may be. Lineal succession is *per stirpes*, and not *per capita*. For, "since (*a*) benefits are derived from the great-grandson, as well as from the son, the term son extends to the great-grandson; for as far as that degree, descendants equally confer benefits by presenting oblations of food in the prescribed form of half-monthly obsequies."

With regard to illegitimate sons it is an established rule that in the three higher classes they do not inherit, but are entitled to maintenance only. With regard to the illegitimate sons of Sudras, the Calcutta High Court holds that they are entitled to inherit if born of a female slave, founding the rule on passages of the Dayabhaga to that effect (*b*). The Bombay High Court regards slave as meaning a kept concubine, and so held in several cases (*c*). The Madras (*d*) and Allahabad (*e*) High Courts uphold the heritable right of Sudra illegitimate sons; and so does the Privy Council (*f*). The extent of the illegitimate son's right seems to be that he only succeeds to his father. He has no claim to succeed to his father's collaterals either by survivorship or by inheritance. The only case in which he takes by survivorship is to his joint brothers; or, in other words, bastards succeed to each other. Again, he only takes half the share that a legitimate son would take, the other half going to increase the shares of the legitimate sons, if any, or in their absence it goes to the next heir, who would have been excluded altogether by a legitimate son. The only case in which he takes the whole estate is where there is no other heir.

(*a*) Dayabhaga, Chap. XI., s. I., v. 34.
(*b*) Kirpal Narain *v.* Sukurmoni, I. L. R. 19 Cal., 91.
(*c*) Sadu *v.* Baiza, I. L. R. 4 Bomb., 37, and cases there cited.
(*d*) Brindavana *v.* Radhamani, I. L. R. 12 Mad. 72, 86.
(*e*) Hargobind *v.* Dharam Singh, I. L. R. 6 All., 329.
(*f*) Inderun *v.* Ramasawmy, 13 Moore, I. A., 159.

The next rule is also in the language of Menu (*a*):—"To the nearest sapinda, male or female, after him in the third degree the inheritance next belongs." This points to collateral succession; but before we reach that branch of the subject there are other persons in the direct line of the deceased whose position in the order of succession must be ascertained. These are the widow, the daughter, the daughter's son, the father and the mother.

The widow's place in the Mitakshara order of succession has already been described; her right by inheritance is the same as under the Dayabhaga, but it only applies to her husband's separate estate. As regards his joint estate, his coparceners' right by survivorship is paramount to the widow's right by inheritance, and excludes it. The Dayabhaga bases her right to succeed upon the principles of spiritual benefit.

She is postponed to sons, grandsons, and great-grandsons, because she performs acts spiritually beneficial to her husband from the date of her widowhood, and not like them from the moment of birth. But she succeeds, failing male issue, because she "rescues her husband from hell;" and since her husband shares the fruits of her virtue or her vice, therefore it is for his benefit that his wealth should devolve on her.

The widow's claim to succeed to her husband's estate, in preference to brothers, according to the Dayabhaga, is clear, whether the property is divided or undivided; and was recognised by judicial decision (*b*) as early as 1801.

Her right, however, in either school is strictly confined to the property of which her husband was at his death the lawful owner. No right which would have accrued to him had he lived longer ever passes to his widow.

Where there are several widows they all inherit jointly, the last survivor taking the whole, the succession opening to

(*a*) 9 Menu, v. 187.

(*b*) Radhachurn Roy *v.* Kissenchund Roy, 1 Sel. Rep. 33, (new ed.) 44.

the reversionary heirs of the husband at the death of the last survivor. The elder widow has the right of managership, but the rights of enjoyment are equal. The widows cannot divide their title and hold each a separate share by a separate title, but they can divide the enjoyment. Each widow can alienate her widow's estate, but the rights both of the other widows if they survive and of the reversionary heirs cannot be prejudiced thereby (*a*).

Chastity is a condition precedent to the widow taking by inheritance; the unchaste wife is disqualified. But when once the widow's estate has vested, subsequent unchastity does not operate to divest it. This was settled after considerable conflict of authority in the case of Kery Kolitani *v.* Moneeram (*b*), the decision in which was affirmed by the Privy Council.

Although unchastity does not work a forfeiture of the widow's estate, an unlawful second marriage does. The reason probably is that the widow takes her husband's estate during widowhood. Where local or caste custom allows such marriage forfeiture is not always enforced (*c*). Act XV. of 1856 legalises the re-marriage of widows, but prescribes by sec. 2 the extinction of her interest in her husband's estate. No forfeiture is incurred under the Act unless the marriage is legalised by the Act, in which case it is legalised subject to the condition of the widow's right being thereby determined. If the marriage were lawful independently of the Act, then its provisions do not apply to the case. Again, the Act only forfeits her existing vested rights: those which accrue to her after her second marriage, *e.g.* from her son by her first husband, are not within the forfeiture prescribed by the Act (*d*).

(*a*) Janokinath *v.* Mothuranath, I. L. R. 9 Cal., 580 (F. B.).
(*b*) 13 B. L. R. 1, affirmed L. R. 7 Ind. App., 115.
(*c*) Har Saran Das *v.* Nandi, I. L. R. 11 All., 330.
(*d*) Akora *v.* Boreani, 2 B. L. R., A. C. J., 199.

In default of the widow, the daughters inherit, unless excluded by special local or family custom. Menu and Narada (*a*) say:—"The son of a man is even as himself; and the daughter is equal to the son: how, then, can any other inherit his property, notwithstanding the survival of her who is as it were himself?" She inherits because equally with the son she is "a cause of perpetuating the race;" that is, as the author of the Dayabhaga is careful to explain, "such descendants as present funeral oblations."

This is one of the instances in which the Mitakshara lays stress on sapindaship as denoting consanguinity, while the Dayabhaga adheres rigidly to the doctrine of spiritual benefit. The former relies on a text of Vrihashati: "as a son, so does the daughter of a man proceed from his several limbs. How, then, should any other person take her father's wealth?" (*b*) The latter says that (*c*) the daughter can confer great spiritual benefit on her father by giving birth to a son, who will deliver him and his ancestors from hell, and accordingly restricts the right of inheritance to one who is mother of male issue, or is likely to become so; and excludes the childless widow, the barren, or the mother of female issue only. It was for the same reason that he gave priority over her sisters to the maiden daughter, because her marriage might otherwise be delayed on account of her indigence beyond the age of puberty, and thus the salvation of her father's soul, and of that of his ancestors, be brought into peril. The Mitakshara also gives priority to the maiden daughter, simply on the ground of a special text of Catyayana, "in default of the widow, let the daughter inherit, if unmarried." If, however, the competition be between an unprovided and

(*a*) Dayabhaga, Chap. XI., sec. 2, verse 1.

(*b*) Mitakshara, Chap. II., sec. 2, verse 2.

(*c*) Dayabhaga, Chap. XI., sec. 2, verses 3, 7.

an enriched daughter, the unprovided one inherits, but on failure of her, the enriched one succeeds.

The daughter stands on the same footing as the widow as regards unchastity (*a*): except that in Bombay it has been held that she is not excluded thereby from taking her father's estate (*b*). She is also excluded by any disqualification which would exclude a male.

The extent of the estate which she takes is exactly similar to the widow, that is, she takes a widow's estate, the succession at her death passing to the heirs of the last full owner (*c*): except in Bombay, where she takes absolutely (*d*). In that part of India the rule seems to be that women who have married into the gotra of the last full owner take a widow's estate; those who have married or may marry into another *gotra* take absolutely. His widow, mother, grandmother, therefore, take a widow's estate; his daughter, sister, and niece take absolutely. The sister does not succeed anywhere in India, except in Bombay, unless by custom; and in Bombay she takes absolutely.

Precedence amongst daughters differs according to the schools. Under the Bengal school it is (1) the maiden daughter, (2) the daughter who has or is likely to have male issue, the barren or sonless daughter being excluded. Under the Benares school the order is (1) the maiden, (2) the married and indigent daughter, (3) the married and wealthy. In Mithila it is (1) the maiden, (2) the married without distinction, either as to her issue or possessions.

Where there are several daughters of the same class they will take jointly in the manner before described with respect

(*a*) Kery Kolitani *v.* Moneeram, L. R. 7 I. A., 115.

(*b*) Advyapa *v.* Rudrava, I. L. R. 4 Bomb., 104.

(*c*) Chotaylall *v.* Chunnolall, L. R. 6 I. A., 15.

(*d*) Lulloobhoy *v.* Cassibai, L. R. 7 I. A., 212.

to widows; except in Bombay, where they take separate shares absolutely (*a*).

The general rule is that the daughter only succeeds to her own father, that is, in her capacity as daughter. She does not succeed to her brother, or to her father's brother, or to her paternal grandfather. In Bombay females are admitted with great laxity. They come in on the ground of consanguinity—including the granddaughter, brother's daughter, and sister's daughter, and even daughters of descendants and collaterals to, it is said, the sixth degree. The Dayabhaga limits them by requiring connection through the obsequies, which practically excludes all but the widow, daughter, mother, and paternal grandmother. The Mitakshara limits them by requiring them to be of the same gotra as the last full owner. Local customs, especially in Oudh and the Punjab, frequently exclude the daughter and her descendants altogether from the list of heirs, in order to preserve the estate in the gotra to which it belongs.

With regard to daughters' sons, the Dayabhaga says (*b*):—"It is the daughter's son who is the giver of a funeral oblation, not his son; nor the daughter's daughter; for the funeral oblation ceases with him." Lineal succession through a daughter therefore terminates with a son; her daughter and her son's son are rigidly excluded. They are not of the same *gotra* with her father; neither are they his *sapindas*. If the daughter has no son, then upon her death, or the death of the last surviving daughter, without male issue, the next reversionary heirs of the father succeed.

The daughter's son occupies an exceptional position. He is a very near sapinda, but he is not a gotraja sapinda, that is, one of the same family with the last full owner. At one time he ranked as a son, but now, according to all the schools, he ranks next to the daughter. It was formerly doubted whether the

(*a*) Bulakhidas *v.* Keshavlal, I. L. R. 6 Bomb., 85.

(*b*) Chap. XI., s. 2, v. 2.

Mithila school recognised his title, Sir William Macnaghten having denied it (*a*). The Sudder Court of Bengal (*b*) decided in his favour, saying, "by approved texts the married daughter and the maiden daughter are preferred to the widowed daughter: the ground of this preference is that the two former may have sons who will benefit their maternal grandfather by the performance of rites. It seems then absurd to hold that an existing daughter's son should be excluded, when his probable birth even would be ground of preference to be shown to his mother."

Daughters' sons are universally recognised as heirs. As long as there is one surviving daughter they do not take. On the death of the survivor they all take *per capita* and *not per stirpes*, differing in this respect from son's sons. They take separate shares in the property as full owners, and not in co-parcenary with rights of survivorship (*c*). No other descendant of a daughter (except her son) has any heritable right, unless in Bombay an exception is made in favour of the daughter's daughter.

The lineal descendants also include the sons of the daughter of a grandson and of a great-grandson in the male line. They are bandhus, that is, sapindas of a different gotra, and offer the pinda to their maternal ancestors in the male line for three degrees, counting from their mother.

When the lineal line in descent from the last full owner is exhausted, the next expedient is to ascend in the same line. Parents are therefore the next in order of succession. The Dayabhaga gives the preference to the father. It says (*d*):—"The father's right of succession should be after the daughter's son, and before the mother; for the father offering two oblations of

(*a*) Principles of Hindu Law, Vol. I., p. 23.

(*b*) Surja Kumari *v.* Gandhrap Singh, 6 Sel rep., 142.

(*c*) Jasoda Koer *v.* Sheo Pershad, I. L. R. 17 Cal., 33.

(*d*) Dayabhaga, Chap. XI., s. 3, v. 3.

food to other manes in which the deceased participates is inferior to the daughter's son, who presents one oblation to the deceased, and two to other manes in which the deceased participates; he is preferable to the mother and the rest, because he presents personally to others two oblations in which the deceased participates."

The Mayukha (IV., s. 8, v. 14) takes the same view. And on failure of the father the mother succeeds.

But the Mitakshara, less influenced by the doctrine of spiritual benefit, and looking rather to proximity in blood relationship, says (*a*) :—"The father is a common parent to other sons, but the mother is not so; and since her propinquity is consequently greatest, it is fit that she should take the estate in the first instance." "Therefore (*b*), since the mother is the nearest of two parents, it is most fit that she should take the estate. But on failure of her the father is successor to the property."

The Bombay High Court follows the Mitakshara or the Mayukha (*c*), according as either law is applicable.

The mother's title to inherit is not affected by a condition as to chastity except in Bengal. When once the estate is vested in her she does not lose it by subsequent unchastity or by re-marriage.

The stepmother does not inherit. She has no consanguinity within the view of the Mitakshara, and no connection through the pinda within the meaning of the Dayabhaga. She is accordingly excluded under both systems (*d*).

In the absence of parents the succession falls to their descendants to the third degree inclusive, and thus we come to collateral succession. Failing all such descendants of parents,

(*a*) Mitakshara, Chap. II., s. 3, v. 3.

(*b*) Verse 5.

(*c*) Balkrishna *v.* Lakshman, I. L. R. 14 Bomb., 605; see 6 Bomb. 541.

(*d*) Lala Joti *v.* Durani, B. L. R. supp. vol., 67.

the inheritance again ascends to the grandparents, and in their absence falls to their descendants to the third degree inclusive before it reascends to the great-grandparents. The Mitakshara again gives the preference to the grandmother and great-grandmother over the grandfather and great-grandfather.

CHAPTER XX.

On Collateral Inheritance.

Brothers—Of the whole blood—Of the half blood—Doctrine of representation does not apply to collaterals—Degree is preferred to line—Collateral succession is per capita—Sons of the whole brothers—Sons of the half brothers—Father's daughter's son—Descendants of the grandfather—Exclusion of women from collateral succession—Sisters are heirs in Bombay—Priority of claim as amongst Bandhus—Conflicting doctrines of the Dayabhaga and Mitakshara on this point—Bandhus *ex parte paternâ*—Bandhus *ex parte maternâ*—Priority amongst saculyas—Amongst samanodakas—Escheat.

Thus far the only material difference between the schools has been in the order of precedence amongst daughters and the priority as between parents, according as the idea of consanguinity or of connection by funeral oblations predominated in the meaning of the word sapinda.

Next to parents brothers succeed. Under the Mitakshara joint brethren succeed by survivorship, separated brethren alone succeed by inheritance. Priority between them is determined by the text "to the nearest sapinda the inheritance next belongs" (*a*), which is again explained as referring to blood relationship, so that brethren of the whole blood take in priority to those of the half blood. Under the Dayabhaga the same rule holds good, for the brothers of the whole blood offer oblations to three generations in the lines of both parents, while those of the half blood only offer to the paternal ancestors.

(*a*) Chap. II., sec. 4, v. 5.

A curious further distinction is introduced in Bengal which could not apply under the Mitakshara, viz., that where brethren of the half blood are joint with the deceased they share equally with brethren of the whole blood who are separated from him. Formerly, on the authority of Sir W. Macnaghten (*a*), it was thought that priority as amongst those of the whole or half blood respectively was determined by their being joint or separate. But that view is abandoned (*b*).

In collateral succession, therefore, the whole blood takes precedence of the half blood. A further rule is that degree takes precedence of line. There is no representation. Brothers take *per capita*, not *per stirpes*. Nephews do not succeed as representing their fathers. All nephews are excluded so long as there is one surviving brother. At his death they take *per capita*.

The reason is again drawn from the principle upon which the Dayabhaga uniformly insists, viz., that the order of succession is regulated by the degree in which spiritual benefits are conferred. "The brother," it says (*c*), "confers benefits on the deceased owner by offering three funeral oblations to his father and other ancestors in which the deceased participates; and he occupies his place as presenting three oblations to the maternal grandfather and the rest, which the deceased was bound to offer; and he is therefore superior to the brother's son, who has not the same qualifications." A nephew (*d*) whose father is living is excluded, because until his father's death he is incompetent to offer oblations; a nephew whose paternal uncle is living is excluded, because such uncle can confer greater benefits.

It must be remembered that if one brother survives and takes the whole estate, the heritable right of the nephews of the last

(*a*) Principles of Hindu Law, p. 26.

(*b*) Sheo Soondary *v.* Pirthee Singh, L. R. 4 I. A., 147.

(*c*) Chap. XI., s. 5, v. 3.

(*d*) See 23 S. W. R., p. 274.

owner is gone. The estate vests in such surviving brother. He becomes a fresh stock of descent, and on his death the estate will pass to his sons or other next heirs.

Then with regard to the inheritance of the brother's sons, upon the question of the whole or the half blood, the High Court of Bengal (*a*) has ruled that there was no analogy between whole and half brothers on the one side and their respective sons on the other; and that all the authorities were agreed that when the succession devolves on nephews the sons of the whole brothers peremptorily excluded the sons of the half brothers. The reason is, as given in the Dayabhaga (*b*), that the son of the half brother gives oblations to the father of the late owner together with his own grandmother, to the exclusion of the mother of the late owner; he is therefore inferior to the son of the whole brother who gives oblations to both the father and the mother of the deceased proprietor.

Next to brother's sons, *i.e.*, father's grandsons, the brother's grandsons, *i.e.*, father's great-grandsons (the same distinction being observed as between the whole and the half blood), are the next in order of precedence. They come in under the Dayabhaga as the next sapindas. In the Mitakshara brothers' sons are held by the Bengal Courts to include the grandsons, though the latter are not specifically mentioned (*c*). But in Madras it is ruled to the contrary (*d*).

On failure of the father's descendants in the male line down to the brother's grandson, the property devolves on the father's daughter's son in like manner as it descends to the owner's daughter's son. He terminates the list of those who offer

(*a*) Kylas Chunder Sircar *v.* Gooroo Churn Sircar, 3 S. W. R., p. 43; affirmed 6 S. W. R., 93.

(*b*) C. XI., sec. 6, par. 2; and see Mitakshara, Chap. II., s. 4, v. 7.

(*c*) Kureem Chand Gurain *v.* Oodung Gurain, 6 S. W. R., 158; and see 14 S. W. R., 208.

(*d*) Suraya Bhukta *v.* Lakshminarasamma, I. L. R. 5 Mad., 291.

M

oblations to the father, or at least of those who are enumerated in the order of succession. But the father's son's daughter's son and the father's grandson's daughter's son are also sapindas, and although they are not enumerated in the list of heirs given by Jimutavahana, yet according to the principle upon which recent decisions have been based they would probably be held entitled to succeed in the absence of all nearer heirs. Under the Mitakshara, though heirs, they would, as belonging to a different gotra, be postponed till all heirs, however distant, in the same gotra are exhausted.

Having thus exhausted the list of heirs who derive their right of succession by virtue of the oblations which they offer to the father of the deceased proprietor, the grandfather becomes the person principally considered as the object of funeral oblations (*a*). Jimutavahana says that the succession of his lineal descendants, including his daughter's son, must be understood in a similar manner to that observed in calculating the order of succession amongst the father's descendants. According to this principle the grandfather would be the first in the list, and then the grandmother, next his sons, *i.e.*, the paternal uncles of the deceased proprietor, and so on, till we come to the grandfather's great-grandsons. But Srikrishna Tarkalankara places the grandfather and grandmother last in this branch of the tree of inheritance.

The succession amongst sapindas would finally be traceable from the great-grandfather of the deceased proprietor in a similar manner to that which is observed in tracing succession through the grandfather.

There still remain two principles to be attended to in reference to collateral succession: (1) the entire exclusion of women; (2) the difference of opinion between the Mitakshara and the Dayabhaga in reference to the priority of claim on the part of

(*a*) Dayabhaga, Chap. XI., s. 6, v. 9.

bandhus, that is those heirs, very limited in number, who trace through a female, and therefore belong to a different gotra from that of the deceased.

On the first point, sisters are not enumerated in the order of succession either in the Dayabhaga or in the Mitakshara according to its proper construction. And it has been consistently held by the Courts that under those schools she does not succeed to her brother. Females, though related as sapindas, are generally excluded from the inheritance. "A woman," says Baudhayana, "is not entitled to the heritage, for females and persons deficient in an organ of sense or member are deemed incompetent to inherit." The succession of the widow, the daughter, the mother, and the paternal grandmother takes effect under express texts without any contradiction to this maxim. Although the daughter is admitted, the sister and the son's daughter are both excluded. The special texts are defended upon the doctrine of a spiritual benefit to the deceased conferred by the persons to whom they apply; but nevertheless it must be recollected that females are as a class disqualified by their sex to perform the religious ceremonies prescribed by the Hindu shasters, in order to secure the spiritual welfare of the deceased. The general character of Hindu succession, according to the latest development of its doctrines, is adverse to the heritable rights of women; the four exceptions being the result of express authority in their favour.

In Bombay, however, sisters are heirs to their brothers. The Mayukha favours their right next in order after the paternal grandmother (*a*). The Privy Council upheld their right in priority to nephews (*b*). The Madras High Court has also held in their favour, departing from the usual view taken of

(*a*) Chap. IV., s. 8, v. 19.

(*b*) Vinayesk *v.* Luxoomeebaee, 3 S. W. R. P.C., 41.

the Mitakshara (*a*). Half sisters are postponed to sisters of the whole blood, and stepsisters are excluded.

On the second point, with reference to the position of bandhus, there is a broad difference between the Dayabhaga and Mitakshara systems. The definition of them is the same in both systems, viz., that they are sapindas sprung of a different family from the deceased, that is, they include all in the table of succession who trace their connection with him collaterally through a female. The radical difference between them is that the Dayabhaga allows them to come in along with sapindas of the same family; while the Mitakshara postpones them at least till all the agnate sapindas are exhausted, and at one time it was contended that even more remote agnates would take in preference to bandhus.

Thus, if the lineal descendants of a deceased fail, and we descend from, first, the father and then the grandfather in collateral lines to three generations, whenever a female appears she is omitted from the table of inheritance, but her son steps into her place as a bandhu. The Dayabhaga says that he offers oblations to his maternal ancestors, who are, some of them, the same as those of the deceased. Accordingly he is entitled to inherit, and his place is next to his mother's brother. In each branch of the pedigree the agnates take precedence of the cognates or bandhus, but cognates in a nearer branch take precedence of agnates in a more distant branch. Those in the same branch offer the same number of oblations to the common ancestor, and therefore take precedence of those in a more distant branch who offer a less number. As between heirs in the same branch or degree, those who offer to paternal ancestors are preferred to those who offer to maternal ancestors.

Similarly, those who offer to the deceased's paternal ancestors take precedence of all who offer only to his maternal ancestors.

(*a*) Kutti Ammal *v.* Radakristna, 8 Mad. H. C. R., 88; but see I. L. R. 13 Mad., 10, and 14 Mad., 149.

His maternal uncle, for instance, does not take till his own sapindas are exhausted; and, accordingly, bandhus *ex parte paternâ* are preferred to bandhus *ex parte maternâ.*

Proximity of relationship and not the superior efficacy of their oblations is the ground of precedence amongst bandhus under the Mitakshara. Those *ex parte paternâ* exclude those *ex parte maternâ.* The nearer branch excludes the more distant; the nearer degree excludes the more distant. The sister's son excludes the aunt's son (*a*); the maternal uncle excludes the maternal aunt's son (*b*). The decided preference of the agnates over the cognates shown by the Mitakshara led at one time to the doctrine that even if all agnatic sapindas were exhausted, an agnatic saculya would nevertheless take precedence of a bandhu. But a Full Bench of the High Court in Bengal (*c*) overruled this doctrine, and places the bandhus or cognate sapindas next after all the agnatic sapindas are exhausted, and before resort is had to the agnatic saculyas.

After the sapindas are exhausted, including those sprung from a different family, the next in order are the *Saculyas,* or relatives connected through the medium of divided oblations. Jimutavahana mentions as belonging to this class (*d*) "the grandson's grandson or other descendant within three degrees reckoned from him; or the offspring of the grandfather's grandfather or other remote ancestor." Those who are connected by participating in oblations appear to be those who are connected by either giving or receiving oblations from the same person instead of, like sapindas, mutually giving or receiving from one another. The deceased owner gave oblations to his three ancestors, they in their lifetime gave to ancestors who included the fifth, sixth, and seventh in ascent.

(*a*) 22 Suth. W. R., 264.
(*b*) I. L. R. 5 Bomb., 597.
(*c*) I. L. R. 9 Cal., 563.
(*d*) Dayabhaga, Chap. XI., s. 6, v. 21.

These last three, therefore, are saculyas of the deceased with their descendants in collateral branches to the third generation; so also are the three next in descent from his great-grandson (*a*).

The next class of heirs are the *Samanodakas*, or those connected by libations of water. They are considered to be included in the term *saculyas* (*b*). Such relationship extends to the fourteenth person, conformably with a text of Vrihat Menu. But the relation of *Samanodakas*, or those connected by libations of water, cease with the fourteenth person.

The old authorities provide for the succession of strangers on total failure of heirs. But the modern authorities establish the title of the Crown by escheat whenever that event occurs (*c*).

(*a*) See Dayabhaga, Chap. XI., s. I, v. 38.

(*b*) Dayabhaga, Chap. XI., s. 6, v. 23.

(*c*) Collector of Masulipatam *v.* Cavaly Vencata, 8 Moore, I. A., 500 and see Ranee Sonet Kowar *v.* Himmut Bahadoor, L. R. 3 I. A., 92.

CHAPTER XXI.

ON EXCLUSION FROM INHERITANCE.

Causes of exclusion—Those which spring from a man's conduct—Those which spring from his condition—Effect of deprivation of caste—Regulation VII. of 1832—Act XXI. of 1850—Disability is personal, and is not transmitted.

THE Mitakshara and the Dayabhaga agree in excluding certain persons from all participation in the ancestral estate and from the right of succession by inheritance. In the former we find (*a*): "An impotent person, an outcast and his issue, one lame, a madman, an idiot, a blind man, and a person afflicted with an incurable disease, as well as others (similarly disqualified) must be maintained, excluding them, however, from participation." They are debarred from their shares if their disqualification arose before the division of the property, but one already separated from his co-heirs is not deprived of his allotment. And the latter treatise is to the same effect (*b*).

Two causes of exclusion are here indicated: first, those which spring from a man's own conduct and lead to his expulsion from caste and consequent deprivation of his right of succession; and, secondly, those which are derived from a man's natural state or condition, disqualifying him for the performance of those spiritual acts which are to benefit the soul of the deceased.

So far as offences have been expiated by penance and the degradation from caste removed, the impediment to succession

(*a*) Mitakshara, Chap. II., s. 10, v. 1.

(*b*) Dayabhaga, Chap. V., v. 11.

is also removed. Rights of inheritance, however, are not permitted to be affected by deprivation of caste, Regulation 7 of 1832 (Bengal Code) and Act XXI. of 1850 having been passed to render inoperative any provision of Hindu law to that effect.

It is therefore important to show that the disability to inherit arises from other causes than the degradation from caste. The incontinence of a wife will forfeit her right of succession to her husband's estate; so also incurable and congenital blindness, deafness, dumbness. Insanity also at the date when the succession opens will exclude. In all these cases there is disability to offer the funeral oblations.

This disability to inherit is purely personal. Its effect is, if the disqualified person is living at the date when the succession opens, to let in the next heir. If the disqualified person died before the succession opened, a right to inherit would have been transmitted through him to his issue. The forfeiture of an estate once vested is not incurred by disqualification supervening; and similarly although a right to inherit would revive if the disqualification were removed, still if the estate had previously vested elsewhere the person in whom it had vested could not be deprived of it (*a*).

(*a*) Kalidas Das *v.* Krishan Chandra Das, 2 Beng. L. R. F. B., 103.

INDEX.